教育部人文社会科学研究青年项目
"英语中汉语借词的源流与发展"(批准号:12YJC740128)

# The Origins and Development of Chinese Loanwords in English

# 英语中汉语借词的源流与发展

杨 彬 著

山东大学出版社

**图书在版编目(CIP)数据**

英语中汉语借词的源流与发展/杨彬著. —济南:山东大学出版社,2016.9
ISBN 978-7-5607-5613-4

Ⅰ.①英… Ⅱ.①杨… Ⅲ.①英语-外来语-借词-研究 Ⅳ.①H313.5

中国版本图书馆 CIP 数据核字(2016)第 226062 号

责任策划:王　潇
责任编辑:王　潇
封面设计:张　荔

---

出版发行:山东大学出版社
社　址　山东省济南市山大南路 20 号
邮　编　250100
电　话　市场部(0531)88364466
经　销:山东省新华书店
印　刷:沂南县汶凤印刷有限公司
规　格:720 毫米×1000 毫米　1/16
11.5 印张　145 千字
版　次:2016 年 9 月第 1 版
印　次:2016 年 9 月第 1 次印刷
定　价:25.00 元

---

# 前言

语言不是存在于真空当中的,语言之间存在各种接触。当语言使用者将其他语言中的成分并入到自己的语言形式中时,语言借用就发生了。最容易被借用的语言成分是词。借词是一种常见的语言现象,也是词汇学研究的重要内容之一。

英语是一个包容性很强的语言,英语词汇中有相当数量的来自其他语言的借词。英语中出现汉语借词已经有一千多年的历史了,但相对于拉丁语、德语、法语等欧洲语言对英语词汇的贡献来说,从汉语借入英语的词汇数量较少。也是由于这个原因,西方学者对汉语借词的相关研究成果不多。而国内的借词研究又是以汉语中的英语借词为主,对于英语中汉语借词的研究虽有关注,但简单举例的多,追根溯源的少,一些问题尚未达成共识。

本书旨在对英语中汉语借词的来源及发展状况做一个梳理和分析。借词是一个动态的概念,一个演进的过程,可分为临时借词、阶段性借词、永久性借词。临时性借词指的是为了表达上的方便,将外语中的某一词语临时借来,仅为当前表达目的服务。阶段性借词指的是某些词语自被临时性引入以来,在一段时间内经常被继续使用,大众对其的熟知度逐渐加强。永久性借词指的是进入某种语言有很长的历史,已经被同化和吸纳的词语,一般使用者往往忽略其词源。从历时的角度看,已经被英语词典所收录,广泛使用的汉语借词在当初刚刚进入英语时也是临时性借用，随着使用频率的增加，才逐渐完成词汇化过程。借词的形式有多种。本书中讨论的汉语借词既包括单个的词，也包括词组和固定表达式；既有音译借词，也含翻译借词、混合借词等。书中根据汉语与英语接触的历史，将英语中汉语借词的发展大致分为四个阶段，描述了每个阶段的特点并对一些典型借词的词源进行了讨论。源自其他语言的词语进入某一语言时通常先由外来语词典收录，进而再出现在通用词典中。书中对五本英文的外来语词典及牛津英语词典中标注汉语词源的词语做了考察。目前，英语已成为全球性的通用语言，世界英语的概念已被广泛接受。在全球化的浪潮中，中国跟世界各国的交流进一步深入，特别是近年来突飞猛进的中国经济和日益增强的综合国力让世界更加关注中国的发展，一批反映中国社会和文化的特色词汇出现在英语媒体中，成为形成中的中国英语的重要特征，也显示着汉语借词的发展趋势。

在写作过程中，作者查阅参考了国内外诸多专家学者的论著，在此表示衷心的感谢。感谢导师汪榕培先生引领我进入英语词汇学研究的广阔天地，先生一直对我关爱有加，对他的感激之情无以言表。

本书为教育部人文社会科学研究青年基金项目“英语中汉语借词的源流与发展”的主要成果。由于作者的研究水平及精力有限，加之缺少第一手的文献资料，本书未能对汉语借词进行全方位的描述和阐释，有一些词的来源还有待进一步查证。从中外交流的历史中寻找线索，从语言学、历史学、社会学、文化学等领域挖掘证据，将是本课题进一步研究的方向。书稿虽经反复修改和校对，仍会有讹误及失当之处，欢迎广大读者批评指正。

2016 年 4 月于泉城

# Contents

# Chapter 1 Introduction

All languages, no matter how small, encapsulate knowledge about the world and everything in it. Language is the instrument through which we make sense of the world and communicate our knowledge of it. Languages do not exist in a vacuum. There is always linguistic contact between groups. When a community of speakers incorporates some linguistic elements into its language from another language, linguistic borrowing occurs. Such transferences are most common in the realm of vocabulary, where words may come and disappear with little consequence for the whole system of the language. The processing of borrowing words from another language is called lexical borrowing. The words borrowed are called loanwords. "Loan" and "borrowing" are of course metaphors, because there is no transfer from one language to another, and no "returning" words to the source language. The process of borrowing "is one of the most frequent ways of acquiring new words, and speakers of all languages do it" (Trask, 1996: 18).

Loanwords have long been recognized as important linguistic phenomena. As the renowned linguist Jespersen (1922: 211) put it, "[t]he question of the value of loanwords can not be dismissed offhand, as the 'purists' in many countries are inclined to imagine, with the dictum that foreign words should be shunned like the plague, but requires for its solution a careful consideration of the merits and demerits of each separate foreign term viewed in connection with the native resources for expressing a particular idea."

"No language is entirely free from borrowed words, because no nation has ever been completely isolated" (Jespersen, 1922: 208). English is no exception. English is already the world's universal language. It is used as a second language or foreign language in more and more countries. The world will become by and large bilingual, with people mastering both English and their native/national language (Zuckermann, 2003). English is "a language of immigrants" (Metcalf, 1999: 28), consisting in great part of words that have come into English from other cultures around the world. Borrowing has played a crucial role in the history of the English lexicon—and still does. "One thing is certain: well over 80 percent of the total vocabulary of English is borrowed" (Stockwell & Minkova, 2001: 2). In general English, for example, only 31.8 percent of the 10,000 most frequent words are native or Germanic words in continuous use since Old English times (Stockwell & Minkova, 2001). It is estimated that more than 120 languages have provided vocabulary for modern English. As a result, English boasts its cosmopolitan vocabulary. Some borrowings like *sushi*, *vodka*, *terrine*, or *coup d'etat* stand out to us immediately, but many others are so thoroughly embedded in the everyday language that only specialists are aware of their foreign origin (for example, *cheese*, *inch*, *war*, or even *they*). A recent important collaborative project is the World Loanwords Database project (WOLD). In this project an extended version of the wordlist of the Intercontinental Dictionary Series meaning list has been used as the basis of a wide-ranging cross-linguistic survey of lexical borrowing. As part of this project, Anthony Grant (2009) looked at contemporary British English and found that 41 percent of the meanings in this full meaning list were normally realized by words which can be identified as loanwords. In fact it would be safe to say that it is impossible to communicate effectively in English without using words that were originally borrowed from other languages.

Mountains of literature has been produced on the subject of loanwords. Studies of the origins of English words tend to give detailed lists of words borrowed from Greek and Latin, French, Germanic and Middle Eastern languages among others. They also tend to include quite a number of examples from Eastern languages like Indian, Malay and Japanese. The English vocabulary was deeply influenced by these particular sources. A recent important trend in linguistic research has been to examine lexical borrowing in the context of broader issues of language contact and to attempt to classify the different sorts of linguistic borrowing that typify different sorts of contact situations (Durkin, 2014). "But when it comes to Chinese the inclusions tend to be few indeed" (Chan, 1983: 62).

It was traditionally assumed that Chinese borrowings in English were few. Samuel Johnson's *A Dictionary of the English Language* (1755) included 10 Chinese words (i. e. *bohea*, *china*, *China-orange*, *China-root*, *ginseng*, *junk*, *mandarin*, *silk*, *tea*, *tutenag*). Waller Skeat's *Etymological Dictionary of the English Language* (1888) had 8 Chinese words (i. e. *china*, *Chinese*, *nankeen/nankin*, *tea*, *typhoon*, *junk*, *serge*, *silk*). Serjeantson (1935) listed just 27 items from Chinese. *The Oxford Companion to the English Language* (McArthur, 1992) lists the following words: *china*, *chin-chin*, *chopsticks*, *chopsuey*, *chow chow*, *chowmein*, *fan-tan*, *ginseng*, *gung-ho*, *kaolin*, *ketchup/catsup*, *kowtow*, *kungfu*, *litchi/lichee/lychee*, *loquat*, *mahjong*, *pekoe*, *sampan*, *taichi*, *taipan*, *Tao*, *tea*, *yang*, *yen*, *yin*. In the works of lexicology, words borrowed from Chinese are scarcely mentioned. "*Silk* may ultimately be from Chinese, though there is no known etymon in Chinese languages. Also ultimately from Chinese are *judo*, *tycoon* and *kamikaze*, but they came into English via Japanese" (Jackson & Amvela, 2007: 42). In his *The Origins and Development of the English Language* (2010), Algeo says that other English words from languages spoken in the Orient are comparatively few in number, but some are quite well known. Silk fiber came from China, but the origin of the word *silk* (Old English sioloc or seolec) is unknown. From various dialects of Chinese come *ch'i-kung* (or *qigong*), *feng shui*, *foo yong*, *ginseng*, *gung-ho*, *I-Ching*, *ketchup*, *kowtow*, *kumquat*, *kung fu*, *litchi*, *pongee*, *t'ai chi ch'uan*, *tea* (and its informal British variant *char*), *wok*, *wonton*, and *yin-yang*. *Typhoon* is a remodeling based on a Chinese word meaning "big wind" of an earlier form with roots in Portuguese, Urdu, Arabic, and ultimately Greek, being a word with a very mixed ancestry. Americanisms of Chinese origin are *chop suey*, *chow*, *chow mein*, and *tong* "secret society" (Algeo, 2010: 265).

Among western concerns of Chinese loanwords in English, Cannon's studies (1987, 1988, 1990) give more credit to words of

Chinese origin. According to Cannon (1987), at least 1,191 Chinese items got into English over the past three centuries. His articles were complemented by Moody (1996), who centered on the information provided by *The Oxford English Dictionary* (OED), but also on *Webster's Third New International Dictionary of the English Language*.

Borrowing is a consequence of cultural contact between two language communities. Borrowing of words can go in both directions between the two languages in contact, but often there is an asymmetry, such that more words go from one side to the other. In this case the source language community has some advantage of power, prestige and/or wealth that makes the objects and ideas it brings desirable and useful to the borrowing language community. For the contact of English and Chinese, Chinese has borrowed more words from English. Compared with other languages, Chinese only contributes a small portion in English borrowings.

In China, borrowing of lexical items is an area that has given rise to considerable discussion, but not to systematic study. Scholars are more concerned with the discussion of the influence of English upon Chinese language, trying to explore loanwords from English to Chinese. Some scholars discussed the issue of Chinese loanwords in English and presented some widely acknowledged words (Zheng Shengtao, 1985; Liu Fagong, 1991; Wang Rongpei & Chang Junyue, 2001; Zhang Yi & Cai Jing, 2005; Xu Aijun, 2009; Chen Shengli, 2014). However, in terms of the amount of literature, Chinese loanwords in English have not been given due consideration. "... the subject of lexical borrowing from Chinese into English has not been systematically studied" (Chan & Kwok, 1985: vi).

Although Chinese loanwords didn't bring about huge influence upon the English language compared with European languages, the exploration of Chinese loanwords will illustrate some key aspects of the effects of borrowing on the vocabulary of English over time and show the historical traces of communication between China and English speaking countries. In today's globalization era, English is becoming a world language. English has been and will likely continue to be an integral part of China's reform and modernization process. On the other hand, with the intense communication between China and English speaking countries, more and more Chinese concepts and terms are becoming familiar to English speakers. English vocabulary is being enlarged with Chinese elements due to the economic expansion of China.

This study attempts to discuss the historical development of Chinese loanwords in English. We focus on Chinese words which have entered the vocabulary of English, trying to trace the historical development of them and explore the new trend of Chinese loanwords in the context of World English.

# Chapter 2 Language Contact and Loanwords

## 2.1 Introduction

Language contacts may come in different forms and with different results. They may be short-lived or long-lived. Borrowing and absorption of language elements will bring problems like combined languages, code switching, code-mixing, borrowing, maintenance, interference, and dead language. While linguistic borrowings may occur at any linguistic level (Thomason & Kaufman, 1988), what is most commonly seen is borrowing of language elements, and what is most noticing is borrowing of words. Through stories, songs and histories a language can tell us about the origins, ancestry and important events in the life of a group (Crystal, 2003). The vocabulary of a language reflects the way of life in the culture of the speakers. Lexical borrowing usually occurs when one culture comes into contact with another. Borrowings have long been recognized as important linguistic phenomena that emerge in contexts of language and cultural contact

(Haugen, 1950; Lehmann, 1962; Hockett, 1979). Historical linguists have come to the conclusion that very few languages in the world today are unrelated to any other language as cultural exchange has been an inseparable part of human history.

## 2.2 Language Contact

As Sapir (2002) put it, languages, like culture, are rarely sufficient unto themselves. Languages have been in contact for centuries. Nations of different languages seek contact with each other for many reasons, such as commerce, trade, war, conquest, colonization, immigration and geographical proximity. Such contacts are closely followed by language contact. Language contact may leave influence on both or all languages involved, though the degree of influence cannot always be the same. Different social and cultural contacts may lead to different degrees of language contacts. Various kinds of contacts may lead to various kinds of influence. During the process of language contact, the borrowing language is going to attract various foreign elements, and the product will be either graphic, phonological, morphosyntactic, lexical or syntactic. Generally speaking, the longer the time of contact is, the greater the influence of the language on each other will be; and the more closely related the involved languages are, the easier and greater the influence will be. The most common way that languages influence each other is the exchange of words.

The historical record, together with methods of historical and comparative linguistics, can help us infer which words were borrowed, from what language, and approximately when. On the synchronic level, however, making such inferences can be more difficult, particularly because there is no unequivocal way of deciding when a lexical item from one language, used during discourse in another language, whether by a single speaker, or repeatedly in a community, should be considered a loanword. It may constitute all or part of a code-switch, which is a phenomenon quite distinct from borrowing. It may be a manifestation of incomplete acquisition of one of a bilingual's two languages. It might be a momentary lapse of the type often classified as "interference". Or we might want to characterize it as still another kind of result of language contact (Poplack & Sankoff, 1984).

The extent of lexical borrowing, and the level of contact which drives it, vary hugely from language to language. The extent of language contact influences what loanwords are integrated into the lexicon and why certain words are chosen over others. Table 2.1 is a summary by Thomason (2001: 70).

**Table 2.1 Thomason's (2001) borrowing scale (adapted and abridged)**

| Degree of contact | Scale of lexical borrowing | Borrowers |
|---|---|---|
| Casual | Mostly nouns, some verbs, adjectives and adverbs; non-basic vocabulary | No fluency in source language required; few bilinguals |
| Slightly more intense | Nouns, verbs, adjectives, adverbs, conjunctions, adverbial particles; non-basic vocabulary | Reasonably fluent bilinguals forming minority of borrowing language speakers |

| Degree of contact | Scale of lexical borrowing | Borrowers |
|---|---|---|
| More intense | Nouns, verbs, adjectives, adverbs, derivational affixes; basic and non-basic vocabulary | More bilinguals, social factors favor borrowing |
| intense | Heavy borrowing of all vocabulary | Extensive bilingualism, social factors strongly favor borrowing |

All languages have more or less borrowed words in their vocabulary. "The vocabulary turnover in English has been quite remarkable; etymologically, the English we speak now does not look like the offspring of Old English at all. More than 80 percent of the vocabulary used a thousand years ago has been replaced with words borrowed since the Norman Conquest" (Stockwell & Minkova, 2001: 46).

English has gone through many periods in which large numbers of words from other languages were borrowed. These periods coincide with times of major cultural contact between English speakers and those speaking other languages. The waves of borrowing during periods of especially strong cultural contacts are not sharply delimited, and can overlap.

The long documented history of English includes contact with languages in a variety of contexts, including: the dissemination of Christian culture in Latin in Anglo-Saxon England, and the interactions of French, Latin, Scandinavian, Celtic, and English during the Middle Ages; exposure to languages throughout the world during the colonial era; and the effects of using English as an international language of science. The phenomenon of homonymy in English is partly caused by the wide contact of English with other languages. For instance, *rest* in *to take a rest* is a word of native Germanic origin, but *rest* in *the rest of* is a loanword of French origin. Many of the words taken over from other languages are indeed extremely interesting from many points of view. One is that these words came from nations that England had commercial and other relations with. Attention has been called to the musical terms derived from Italian, and a similar list of terms of architecture and art in general taken from the same language (e. g. *colonnade*, *cornice*, *corridor*, *grotto*, *niche*, *parapet*, *pilaster*, *profile*; *miniature*, *fresco*, *improvisatore*, *motto*) could be made the basis of an interesting chapter in a history of European civilization. A considerable number of military words (e. g. *alarm* or *alarum*, *cartridge*, *corporal*, *cuirass*, *pistol*, *sentinel*) carry us back to wars between Italy and France.

According to Weinreich (1953), language contact assumes face-to-face contact between speakers of two or more languages and thus bilingual speakers are a necessary prerequisite for any occurrence of large-scale contact. However, this restricted definition cannot explain the case of Chinese-English language contact because of its two distinctive characteristics. For one thing, Chinese-English contact does not take place in a bilingual environment. For another, Chinese speakers have more contact with written English than spoken English. Therefore, a broader understanding of language contact is quite necessary (Guo Hongjie, 2005: 3).

## 2.3 Defining Loanwords

### 2.3.1 What is a loanword

In linguistics, the term "borrowing" describes a process in which one language replicates a linguistic feature from another language, either wholly or partly. The metaphorical use of the word "borrowing" to describe this process has some well-known flaws: nothing is taken away from what is termed the donor or "lending" language, and there is no assumption that the "borrowing" or "loan" will ever be returned. Also, the language from which the words originate does not actually lose the words, which still form part of its vocabulary. However, the term "borrowing" has been firmly entrenched in linguistics as the usual term to describe this process since the 19th century, to the extent that most linguists no longer even think of it as a metaphor (Durkin, 2014: 3).

The term loanword has the vaguest and most general meaning. It has been defined in various ways.

Following Algeo (1990: 409), we can see "the process of borrowing as correlated with cultural contact and innovation". When speakers imitate a word from a foreign language and at least adapt or import its sound or grammar to their native ways, the process of borrowing is taking place and the words herewith borrowed is a loanword.

Campbell & Mixco (2007: 110) defines loanword as "a word in a language that is borrowed from another language, or, more specifically, a word or expression in a recipient language that through the process of borrowing has been borrowed, imported or copied from a donor language through bilingual usage during language contact. For example, English *pork* is a loanword from French *porc* (pork), and was not a word in the English language until after it was taken over from French. Loanwords may undergo varying degrees of naturalization in their accommodation of the phonological, morphological, syntactic or semantic patterns of the recipient language, and may reveal patterned deviations from native structure that can serve as clues to their foreign origin and even their specific original source when the comparative method is applied".

In *The Longman Dictionary of Language Teaching and Applied Linguistics* edited by Richards & Schmidt (2010), borrowing/loanword is defined as "a word or phrase which has been taken from one language and used in another language. For example, English has taken *coup d'état* (the sudden seizure of government power) from French, *al fresco* (in the open air) from Italian and *moccasin* (a type of shoe) from an American Indian language. When a borrowing is a single word, it is called a loanword. Sometimes, speakers try to pronounce borrowings as they are pronounced in the original language. However, if a borrowed word or phrase is widely used, most speakers will pronounce it according to the sound system of their own language. For example, French *garage* has different pronunciation in British English and American English".

*The International Encyclopedia of Linguistics* defines loanwords as "vocabulary whose basic form and meaning are taken directly from another language, then integrated with lesser or greater fidelity into the phonological and grammatical systems of the matrix language" (Haugen & Mithun, 2003: 243).

"Borrowing" seems to be the most commonly used term to describe the process in which a language takes words from another language, and "loanword" is the name given to those words that have been taken in this way. From a different point of view, borrowing and loaning are both sides of the same phenomenon. From the perspective of the recipient language, the words are borrowed; from the viewpoint of the source language, the words are loaned (Doi, 2014).

Loanwords are sometimes used interchangeably with "foreign words". A foreign-word has been adapted into the native system, with a stable spelling and pronunciation (native or exotic), or a compromise has been made by translating all or part into a native equivalent.

The concept of loanword is distinctive from foreignism. According to Richards & Schmidt (2010), foreignism refers to a person's use of a word or expression from another language when speaking one's native language in order to create a special effect or to indicate special knowledge. For example, when a speaker of Indonesian uses words from Dutch or English to indicate their familiarity with those languages or when a speaker of English uses a word from French or German (with a French or German pronunciation), as in "I think he lacks a certain panache."

If loanwords are to be incorporated into the utterances of a new language, they must be fitted into its grammatical structure. This means that they must be assigned by the borrower to the various grammatical classes which are distinguished by his own language. A great number of words in English which once were adopted are now quite indistinguishable from native words. Compounds may be borrowed about as freely as simple stems.

When we speak about the vocabulary (or lexis) of a language, it can be useful to think of a common core of basic. Beyond this we can attempt to identify numerous different vocabularies belonging to different specialisms (e. g. activities, professions), to different functions (e. g. academic discourse), or to different stylistic registers (formal, informal, etc.). In each of these, some words will be frequent and known to most if not all speakers, others will be very rare and restricted to very small numbers of speakers. Borrowed words can belong to any of these categories: some are in everyday use in even the simplest discourse, while others are used only very occasionally in very restricted circumstances and only ever by certain speakers (Durkin, 2014: 19).

#### 2.3.2 Different kinds of loanwords

Lexical borrowing occurs when the lexis of one language exercises an influence on the lexis of another language, with the result that the borrowing language acquires a new word form or word meaning, or both, from the donor language (Durkin, 2014). In terms of the semantic content of loanwords, Algeo (2010) makes a distinction between popular and learned loanwords. "Popular loanwords are transmitted orally and are part of everyday talk. For the most part we do not think of them as different from other English words; in fact, most people who use them are not aware that their origin is foreign. Learned loanwords, on the other hand, owe their adoption to scholarly, scientific, or literary influences. Originally learned words may in time become part of the ordinary, popular vocabulary." (Algeo, 2010: 248)

Words have both a form and a meaning. Either component can be borrowed. Any new form in the borrowing language is then a loanword, and it shows morphemic importation without substitution. The narrow sense of loanwords can be referred to single words. The other main types of lexical borrowing involve borrowing of meaning but not (directly) of word form, and can conveniently be referred to under the cover term semantic borrowing. In some cases the structure of a word in the donor language is replicated by a new word in the borrowing language. This is typically called a loan translation or calque.

Einar Haugen (1950) suggests three major types of borrowing—loanwords, loanshifts and loanblends. Haugen's suggestions for the classification and categorization of linguistic borrowing remain the main point of reference for studies of linguistic borrowings.

The commonest loans are single words: *pizza* (from Italian to English), *babysitter* (from English to French, German, and other languages). Once adopted, loans usually show some adaptation: in sound, French *garage*, variously pronounced in English; in form, English *night* taken into Italian as a clipping of nightclub; in grammar, English nouns borrowed into French and provided with a gender, *la babysitter* (feminine), *le golf* (masculine). Verbs adapt to the morphology of the borrowing language: in German, *babysitten* to babysit, past tense *babysittete*, past participle *gebabysittet*. Occasionally, words are borrowed with a different meaning than the meaning in the source language. Among the most well-known examples of this is the German word *Handy*, which is a borrowing of the English adjective *handy*, but means mobile phone and is thus a noun. Conversely, in English the prefix *über-*, taken from German, is used in a way that it is rarely used in German.

Loanshift results from substitution of native morphemes in a foreign pattern, without the importation of any foreign morpheme. In other words, each morpheme or word is translated into the equivalent morpheme or word in another language. It is also known as loan translation or calque. New expressions are formed by using the morphemes and rules of borrowing language to interpret words of another language. A loan translation may be a word, a phrase, or even a short sentence, for example, *lightning war* is a loanshift from German *Blitzkrieg*, and *beer garden* is a loanshift from German *Biergarten*. The word "loanword" is itself a loanshift (loan translation) of the German word *Lehnwort*.

Loanblend refers to the hybrid form which is made up of part importation and part substitution, i. e. one part of a word is borrowed from a second language and the other part belongs to the speaker's native language. For example, *grüngrocer* in the German spoken in Australia has the first element of German and the second element of English (from greengrocer). 苹果派 in Chinese is from English word *apple pie*.

Another classification is based on the form of loanwords, which is somewhat overlapping with the above classification. They are phonetic loans, semantic loans, graphic loans and hybrids.

Phonetic loans are transcriptions of foreign sounds. This may cause some complications because the two languages are very different in syllable structure. Speakers of one language often have difficulty reproducing the sounds of another language which do not exist in their own. The borrowing of lexical items containing such sounds usually entails adaptation of their pronunciation. An example from English is the anglicization of the "r" sound in word such as *restaurant* borrowed from French. Thus, some borrowings cannot be carried out phoneme for phoneme. This is also similar to the way by which English has borrowed *kowtow* and *chow mein* in Chinese. There are two steps for the adaptation of a Chinese word in English. First, the Chinese sound is replaced by the phonologically or phonetically closest English phoneme. Second, syllable structures, which cannot be allowed in English phonology, are fixed to conform to English phonotactic constraints. There are many cases that the meaning is more easily or effectively expressed through phonetic loans. Semantic loans borrow the meaning of foreign words. The users use native resource to coin a new word, as in the case of 电视 (electric vision) for *television*. Graphic loans borrow the letters of a foreign word directly. Hybrids combine both phonetic loans and the semantic loans.

Each item in the source language has its phonetic shape, written representation, grammatical status and meaning. During the course of importation certain changes may take place causing the loanword to diverge from its source item in many ways (Chan & Kwok, 1985: 79). In the case of words of Chinese origin in the English lexicon, the most obvious change takes place on the orthographical level. Chinese words are written in characters, and when they are used in English, they have to be replaced by sequences of letters of the alphabet. The spelling of each word is meant to suggest a pronunciation close to the pronunciation of the original item. Many transliterations and loan translations have penetrated into English for a long time and somewhat naturalized. These words, based on the morphological rules of English, could develop new forms, such as *Chinatown*, *Sinologist*, *Taoism*, *Mandarin duck*, *Peking opera*, etc.

For the purpose of this study, the concept of "loanword" covers a wide range of vocabulary items, including words that are borrowed from a foreign language either morphologically or phonologically in the forms of direct phonological adaptations, indirect meaningful translations, and native creations describing imported objects.

## 2.4 The Motivation of Lexical Borrowing

### 2.4.1 Need-filing

It is a universal cause of borrowing if we have the need to designate new things, persons, places, and concepts. When a new object or a new concept is introduced from a foreign place to the local vicinity, a new name or referent is needed because there is simply no other available word. Certain categories of words are more commonly borrowed than others, usually words for exotic concepts or ideas. What is "exotic" varies from language to language. For example, "English has borrowed *whisky* from Scots Gaelic, *yogurt* from Turkish, *tomato* from Nahuatl, *sauna* from Finnish, *ukulele* from Hawaiian and *kangaroo* from the Guugu Yimithirr language of Australia. The reason for this is that English speakers had never seen whisky or yogurt or tomatoes or saunas or ukuleles or kangaroos before encountering these things overseas" (Trask, 2007: 159). Other examples of loanwords English are *apartheid* (from Afrikaans), *perestroika* (from Russian), *pyjamas* (from Hindi).

It would appear that quite a number of loans have been adopted because of a certain degree of "need-filling" and the wish to achieve precision in meaning. The "thing" referred to may be new to the English-speaking person. But a real "need" in many cases is augmented, or at least reinforced by a desire to be original and fresh in expression. The use of loanwords will give exotic connotations and a sense of local color.

Certain aspects of Chinese civilization, both material and spiritual, are so different from that of the West that new terms are required to deal with the unique artefacts and concepts. When English-speaking people need to express the "new" referent, they take the English name for the familiar thing and adapt it to fit the new thing by adding a prefix indicative of its Chinese origin. Examples are *Chinese broccoli*, *Chinese cabbage*, *Chinese mushroom*, *Chinese potato* (also known as *Chinese yam*), *Chinese frying pan* (later simplified to *wok*, a phonetic loan) (Chan & Kwok, 1985: 50).

### 2.4.2 Economy

Borrowing is not just a question of filling in a linguistic gap, but also serves other functions. Associated with the need-filling is the concept of linguistic laziness or economy. When a new concept or object is introduced from a foreign culture, the most convenient way is to take over the original name for it. The borrowing is not occasioned by an inherent deficiency in the language itself, but is shown by the ease with which new terms actually are framed for the convenience of communication. Interesting examples may be found in Edward E. Morris's *Austral English: A Dictionary of Australasian Words, Phrases and Usages* (2011). As Morris says in his preface, "Those who, speaking the tongue of Shakespeare, of Milton, and of Dr. Johnson, came to various parts of Australasia, found a Flora and a Fauna waiting to be named in English. New birds, beasts and fishes, new trees, bushes and flowers, had to receive names for general use. It is probably not too much to say that there never was an instance in history when so many new names were needed, and that there never will be such an occasion again, for never did settlers come, nor can they ever again come, upon Flora and Fauna so completely different from anything seen by them before." (Morris, 2011: xii) The gaps were filled partly by adopting words from the aboriginal languages, e. g. *kangaroo*, *wombat*, partly by applying English words to objects bearing a real or fancied resemblance to the objects denoted by them in England, e. g. *magpie*, *oak*, *beech*, but partly also by new English formations.

#### 2.4.3 Prestige

Another important motive of lexical borrowing is social and heavily influenced by perceptions of prestige. Prestigious languages have always been the sources for borrowing. It is more likely that the language of a more advanced, or politically and culturally more dominant and powerful nation is borrowed by the language of a less advanced, or less powerful nation, and the conqueror's language is borrowed by the language of the conquered nation. At any given time in any given place, some languages typically enjoy more prestige than others, and speakers of less prestigious languages are often eager to show off their command of a more prestigious language by introducing some of its words into their own speech.

The reason why English and many other languages borrowed greatly from Latin and Greek is that Latin and Greek had long been considered elegant and prestigious language developing from brilliant cultural backgrounds.

After the Norman conquest of England, Norman French enjoyed far more prestige than English. French was widely learned by upper- and middle-classes Englishmen, and French expressions were interlarded within their speech, such as *picture*, *courage*, *army*, *treasure*, *language*, *female* and *beef*, in many cases these fashionable words simply displaced their native English equivalents. This surge was socially driven. French retained its social cachet, and the use of French expressions was an obvious way of signaling a higher social position. Even in present day English, French-derived vocabulary is often stylistically marked as of a higher register.

Nowadays, English is the most-widely used international language. It penetrates in many arenas of businesses. English words are borrowed into different languages. In the 19th and early 20th centuries, Chinese borrowed massively from English and Japanese. That was mainly because Britain, the United States and Japan were then more advanced than China in science and technology, and in many other fields (Hu Zhaoyun, 2001: 75). Many contemporary Japanese borrowings from English also fall into this category. Japanese words like *oopun* (grand opening), *seeru* (sale), *gihuto* (gift) were borrowed from English even though these concepts were not new in the Japanese culture. English words are still pouring into the Japanese vocabulary in this manner today. Compared with English words which have entered the lexicon of the Chinese language, loanwords from Chinese which have entered the English vocabulary, in various stages of integration, are still very few.

### 2.4.4 Cultural Exchange

Whenever people speaking different languages come into contact, there is a natural tendency for them to seek ways of bypassing the communicative barriers facing them by seeking compromise between their forms of speech. Whatever the degree or nature of contact between neighboring peoples, it is generally sufficient to lead to some kind of linguistic inter-influencing and the simplest kind of influence that one language may exert on another is the borrowing of words (Sapir, 2002).

In some cases, the contact may result in only slight borrowing of vocabulary, while other contact situations may lead to the creation of entirely new languages. Between these two extremes lies a wide range of possible outcomes involving varying degrees of influence by one language on the other. Borrowing can lead to larger extent of mutual influence, interference and understanding between the two different cultures. The production of loanwords has more or less affected the existing vocabulary to a certain extent. More accurately, of course, it is the people speaking the respective languages who have contact with each other and who resort to varying forms of mixture of elements from the languages involved (Winford, 2003).

Loanwords are a common phenomenon in societies with mixed cultures and among cultures in close contact. As Tsou (1975: 446) has pointed out that, "it is generally true that the direction of importation is determined by the donor language exerting cultural domination over the recipient language." Much of the vocabulary of French entered English in the Middle Ages because French was the language of political and social power and the channel through which mainland European culture reached Britain. Much of the vocabulary of Latin entered English during the Renaissance because Latin was the European language of religion, education, and learning. When discussing Chinese loanwords, Moody (1996: 405) suggests that words borrowed from the Mandarin dialect of Chinese typically reflect Chinese "high" culture: terms associated with philosophy, religion, history, politics, art, and literature. Borrowings from the Cantonese dialect include a large number of words for various foods. Finally, the Amoy dialect serves as language source for English names of several kinds of tea—the word tea itself being a borrowing from Amoy.

#### 2.4.5 Openness of language

"The lexis of a language is open to the greatest intrusion from a language in contact." (Kachru, 2005: 104) Lexical borrowing involves two broad categories of factors—internal (linguistic) and external (social and psychological). The external factors initiated by language contact are a powerful promoter of linguistic borrowing, while the role of internal factors can not be ignored. Every language has its own unique characteristics. These are reflected in grammar, phonology, morphology, semantics, syntax and other internal structures. Different languages may thus have different borrowing capabilities, different degree of "openness" to borrowing. Some are liable to borrow, enjoying a much wider range and a larger quantity of borrowing. Some are not. English has been linguistically open to outside influence. Brian Foster (1968: 76) once mentioned, "The English language has always been hospitable to words from other tongues and while it is doubtless true to say that all forms of human speech have to some extent borrowed from outside models, there are grounds for thinking that English is more than usually open to foreign influence as compared with other great languages."

It is sometimes the case in lexical borrowing that the motive is a more complex one. There is usually a mixture of motives. Much depends on the caprice of the users of a language. Individuals may use an exotic expression because it seems to them to be the most suitable term available, the only possible term (with no equivalent in any other language), or the most impressive term. Under some circumstances, people borrow words from other languages, not much motivated by "need", but by a desire for ornamentation and suiting certain stylistic purposes.

## 2.5 Lexical Borrowing as a Process

Lexical borrowing occurs anytime anywhere. So it should be regarded as a process rather than a state. We suggest the concept of loanwords is also dynamic. They are tags of language contact and cultural contact.

Cannon (1992) studied Malayan loanwords and developed a model of the naturalization process. Stage 1: words that are glossed, italicized, or used with quotation marks; stage 2: words that exhibit phonetic, grammatical, syntactic and semantic adaptation; stage 3: words that are recorded in all unabridged dictionaries or that have gained some productivity, but are not yet fully absorbed; stage 4: words that are recorded in almost all of the latest desk dictionaries, carrying various meanings.

However, it is a very rough division, and the distinction between the adjacent stages is blurred and unclear. Cannon (1992) has pointed out himself that the naturalizing process is not something that could be divided up into concrete stages but is a matter of degree. Each word in any given language can be located at a certain point on a continuum, with "totally foreign" at one extreme and "fully incorporated" at the other. And this assumption does not necessarily work for those of other origin. When discussing loanwords from a particular language, generalizations should primarily be based on that single language; loanwords from other languages might behave differently.

Schun Doi (2014: 674) puts forward a three-stage naturalization process of loanwords. In the initial stage, words are paraphrased by easily recognizable words or phrases to guarantee that the foreign words employed are understood. Then, attributive usages appear as a transitional phase towards the more productive stage. To finish the naturalization process, the loanwords acquire greater productivity and in due course achieve the fully incorporated status. These three stages here, again, are not a sequence of sudden jumps and the boundaries are somewhat fuzzy; and thus, drawing distinct lines between the stages is implausible.

The actual process of borrowing is complex and involves many usage events, so we can only guess at the factors that have influenced the form of any given word. Certain assumptions could be made.

First, some speakers of the borrowing language know the source language too, or at least enough of it to utilize the relevant word. They adopt the new word when speaking the borrowing language, because it most exactly fits the idea they are trying to express. If they are bilingual in the source language, which is often the case, they might pronounce the words the same or similar to the way they are pronounced in the source language. Secondly, if they have occasions to repeat it, or if other speakers also start using it, a further substitution of native elements will take place. Thirdly, that if monolinguals learn it, a total or practically total substitution will be made. When more speakers, even people who know little or nothing of the source language understand and use these words, they become conventionalized. Conventionalization is a gradual process in which a word progressively permeates a larger and larger speech community, becoming part of ever more people's linguistic repertoire. In time, they do not perceive the word as a loanword at all. Generally, the longer a borrowed word has been in the language, and the more frequently it is used, the more it resembles the native. However, time is not the sole factor that determines the acceptance of a loanword. For instance, the word *sushi* is first recorded in English in the 1890s, but the earliest examples in print all feel the need to explain what *sushi* is, and it is only in recent decades that it has become ubiquitous, as *sushi* has spread along the high street and into supermarket chiller cabinets in most corners of the English-speaking world. But, commonplace though *sushi* may be today, it hasn't made its way into the inner core of English in the same way as words like *peace*, *war*, *just*, or *very* (from French) or *leg*, *sky*, *take*, or they (from Scandinavian languages). This isn't just because they were borrowed longer ago. It owes a great deal to the different influences that foreign languages have had on the word-stock of English over the centuries.

## 2.6 Summary

Language contact leads to linguistic borrowings from one language to another. Lexical items, as units of meaning, are the linguistic elements most likely to be borrowed. There are various reasons for borrowings and the process of assimilation of these borrowed words could be long or short. The borrowed words or the loanwords could have different forms, including the directly taken word, the literal translation or blending of different elements. Sometimes multi-word phrases could also be borrowed. English has had massive contact with other languages through its history and a large number of words of foreign origins came into its vocabulary. Today English borrows from other languages with a truly global sweep.

# Chapter 3 A Brief History of Chinese Loanwords in English

## 3.1 Introduction

Historically many of the large-scale borrowing situations have been the results of conquest, cultural domination, and great disparity in one or more aspect or level of social development. However, unlike many other aspects in the history of English borrowings, the situation with English borrowing from Chinese is different since there is no contiguous border between China and an English-speaking country and the number of English speakers living in China is relatively small. Although the number of loanwords from Chinese to English is rather low, they should not be neglected. During the long history of interaction between China and western countries, a certain number of words have been adopted in English through various channels.

This chapter attempts to trace briefly the nature of the contact between Chinese and English languages and the types of loans resulting from their contacts. Because documentary record is scarce and few dictionaries consistently give etymological information for all the word entries, some of the discussion is based on indirect source. The focus is on the lexical consequences of historical events and the use of borrowed words.

## 3.2 Major Sources of Loanwords in English

English has borrowed massively from French, Latin, and Greek, significantly from Italian, Spanish, German, Danish, and Dutch, and to varying degrees from every other language with which it has come in contact. The different sources of the English word stock are reflected both grammatically and stylistically in the modern language.

Latin influence on English can be seen in every period of the language's history, though its influence has varied in kind from one period to the next. In earlier periods Latin was the language of literature, science, and religion. During the Old English Period, the vast majority of loanwords were from Latin. Throughout the medieval and early modern periods, Latin was freely used in both written and spoken forms by the learned all over Europe. Ancient Greek supplies English with sets of words that are related to logic, math and philosophy.

Some Celtic loanwords doubtless entered the language during the common Germanic period. Most of the Scandinavian words in Old English do not actually occur in written records until the Middle English period, though undoubtedly they were current long before the beginning of that period. In the later part of the 11th century, the Scandinavians became gradually assimilated to English ways, bringing Scandinavian words with them. Many Scandinavian words closely resembled their English cognates; sometimes, indeed, they were so nearly identical that it is difficult to tell whether a given word was Scandinavian or English.

Borrowing from French has gone on ever since the Middle Ages, though never on so large a scale. The Norman Conquest made French the language of the official class in England. Up to the 13th century, recorded borrowings from French into English are few and were generally restricted to the registers of government (e. g. *country*, *court*, *crime*, *defendant*, *evidence*, *justice*, *obedience*, *service*). From the beginning of the 13th century to the end of the Middle English period, however, French words entered the English lexicon in large numbers. There are also a good many loan translations from French, such as *marriage of convenience* (marriage de conveyance), *that goes without saying* (ça va sans dire), and *reason of state* (raison d'état). Suffice it to say that, as a result of the Conquest, English acquired a new look.

English has taken words from various other European languages as well—through travel, trade, exploration, and colonization. A good many Spanish and a smaller number of Portuguese loanwords entered English between the 16th and 18th centuries (Algeo, 2010: 258). From Italian, English has acquired a good many words, including much of the musical terminology. Dutch and German have contributed a number of words to English, to a large extent via the commercial relationships existing between the English and the Dutch and Flemish-speaking peoples from the Middle Ages on. As early as Old English times, words from the East doubtless trickled into the language, then always by way of other languages. A number of words ultimately Arabic, most of them having to do in one way or another with science or with commerce, came in during the Middle English period, usually by way of French or Latin.

Late Modern period of English is a time of lexical expansion. English speakers continue to borrow words from almost every language spoken upon the earth, although no longer with the frequency characteristic of the Middle Ages and Renaissance. English speakers encountered a wide variety of languages as a result of trade, exploration, and colonization. There has also been a shift in the relative importance of languages from which English borrows. "A study by Garland Cannon of more than a thousand recent loanwords from eighty-four languages shows that about 25 percent are from French; 8 percent each from Japanese and Spanish; 7 percent each from Italian and Latin; 6 percent each from African languages, German, and Greek; 4 percent each from Russian and Yiddish; 3 percent from Chinese; and progressively smaller percentages from Arabic, Portuguese, Hindi, Sanskrit, Hebrew, Afrikaans, Malayo-Polynesian, Vietnamese, Amerindian languages, Swedish, Bengali, Danish, Indonesian, Korean, Persian, Amharic, Eskimo-Aleut, Irish, Norwegian, and thirty other languages." (Algeo, 2010: 267)

English and other European languages are genetically, geographically and culturally related, so the borrowing from these languages is much easier than that from other languages, for example, language of non-Indo-European families such as Chinese, Japanese or Korean which are much less related to English both culturally and geographically (Hu Zhaoyun, 2001:71). In the case of borrowing from Chinese there are a number of complications because the structure of English and Chinese are very different and because of the added complications of dialectal variations (Chan & Kwok, 1985: 67). As the language with the largest number of speakers, Chinese have contributed a number of words into the English language over the past centuries.

In the next section, we will give a brief sketch of the development of Chinese loanwords in the English language. By loanword, we prefer a broadest sense, that is, all words that originated from Chinese, including derivatives and loan translations, will be treated as "Chinese loanwords".

## 3.3 Historical Development of Chinese Loanwords in English

Because word-borrowing is a process that takes a long time, it is hardly possible to decide the actual time in which a certain word was first borrowed into a language. The first quotation in dictionaries might represent the first instances of the words appearing in print. However, it must be noted that loanwords usually do not appear in publication for some time after they are loaned into the conversational context.

The Chinese loans have entered English from different Chinese dialects, which is another factor causing the difficulty of accurate identification of the etymology of certain words. China is an ethnically and linguistically diverse country with 56 ethnic groups and over 80 dialects. *Putonghua* ("standard speech", "common speech"), the standard form based on the dialect spoken in Beijing, is China's official spoken language. *Putonghua* is spoken by an estimated 70 percent of the population, mainly in northern and central China. It is sometimes known to Westerners as *Mandarin*. In addition to the Mandarin dialects, there are six other Chinese dialect groups, spoken mainly in southern and southeastern China. They include the Wu dialects, spoken in the Shanghai-Jiangsu-Zhejiang area, with about 100 million native speakers; the Yue dialects (also known as *Cantonese*), spoken in Hong Kong and Guangzhou, with more than 65 million native speakers; and the Kejia (Hakka) dialects, spoken in southern Fujian and also in Taiwan and by many people of Chinese descent around the world. Two place names which are familiar to a large number of English-speakers are Amoy and Canton. The pinyin rendering of these two city names are Xiamen and Guangzhou respectively. But their older names are better known. Amoy, as a southern trading port, became known to Westerners early. Canton has a more complex and less easily traceable origin. The name is a phonetic corruption of Kwangtung (Guangdong), the province of which Canton is the capital. Its correct name is Kuangchou (Guangzhou). Cantonese is also the most common first language of the majority of the population in Hong Kong. Hong Kong, which was once a colony of the Great Britain, played an important part in communication between China and Western Countries (Chan & Kwok, 1985: 97). Although the Chinese dialects are mutually unintelligible in their spoken forms, they share a common written form. The Chinese written language has existed for more than 3,000 years and has been standardized for more than 2,000 years. It has served as an important social cement, tying together the Chinese people.

We are primarily interested in how contacts between China and the West have resulted in the importation into the English vocabulary of words and expressions of Chinese origin. From a diachronic perspective, roughly we present several stages of Chinese words coming into English: the earlier period, the 16th to the 18th century, the 19th to the beginning of 20th century, and 1949 to the present.

### 3.3.1 The Earlier Period

Early travelers to China have translated some Chinese terms to give readers a sense of the exotic. In their writings, the Chinese regarded themselves as the center of the universe, right in the "middle" of the known world, hence the name 中国 or "Middle Kingdom". Wells Williams in the 19th century named his book on China *The Middle Kingdom*. The Chinese Kingdom is sometimes referred to as "all under heaven", which is a translation of 天下, literally "under the heavens". The Chinese referred to their emperor as 天子, literally the "Son of Heaven" (Chan & Kwok, 1985: 59).

The origin of the English word *China* is a matter of debate. Many people believe that it comes from *Chin* 秦, the name of the first feudal dynasty in ancient China. In the third century B. C. what is now known as China was divided into half a dozen warring feudal states. Then the ruler of the Chin state conquered the rest of the country and assumed the title of "First Sovereign Emperor of Qin" (秦始皇). From 221 BC, a succession of dynasties created China's classical civilization: the Han, the Tang, the Song, the Yuan, the Ming, and the Qing among them. They created a civilization in which art, literature, statecraft, medicine, and technology all thrived. Based on the word *China*, some compounds and derivates were created, such as *Chinamania*, *China bean*, *China-orange*, *Chinaman*, *China rose*, *Chinese jujube*, *Chinese anise*, *Chinese calendar* and so on. Another popular belief is that the name of the country is derived from *china*, meaning porcelain. "OED notes that the term China ware occurs ... earlier than the shortened form China and had at first the literal sense of 'ware from China'." This was soon shortened to China, and began to bear the sense of porcelain, the sense in which it is still used (Chan & Kwok, 1985: 96).

The Chinese did not have much association with the outside world before the Han Dynasty. Among the first patch of Chinese words, *silk* was prominent. It was first introduced into Latin (sericus), then to Greek (seres) through the famous *Silk Road*, and then came into English.

The expansion of the *Silk Road* and the initiation of trade with the kingdoms of Central Asia, India, and Persia stimulated culinary exchange. The caravans that carried silk and other precious goods west brought back cucumbers, pomegranates, carrots, walnuts, pistachios, coriander, green peas, spinach, and dates. The trade routes across the seas and over the mountains of Sichuan led to the introduction of South Asian spices; most important were black pepper, cardamom, and nutmeg. Portuguese merchants carried new ingredients from the New World to India and Southeast Asia, and these were brought by boat or caravan to China. Maize (corn) and sweet potatoes became known as peasant foods and live-stock feed (sweet potatoes are also now a popular street snack); peanuts, tomatoes, and particularly chili peppers gained more widespread acceptance. Today, the regions that lie along the main mountain trade route—Sichuan and Hunan provinces—have the highest chili pepper consumption of China (Coe, 2009: 83).

During the Han Dynasty, farmers grew small amounts of wheat and ground it into flour to extract its nutrients. They kneaded wheat flour with water and encompassed a world of new dishes made from this preparation, known as *bing*: steamed breads, grilled flat breads, noodles, and probably some kinds of dumpling (Coe, 2009: 87). From rural villagers to emperors, the taste for *bing* was apparently universal in early medieval China. *Bing* makers sold their products from boats, and vendors hawked steamed breads and noodle soups on the streets. Among the offerings were *mantou*—now, simple steamed breads; then, stuffed with chopped, seasoned meat. Today, similar meat-stuffed dumplings are found from Turkey (manti) to Korea (man-doo). In China, large steamed stuffed breads are now known as *baozi*. Another popular *bing* was *wonton*, a meat or vegetable dumpling enclosed in a thin wrapping. In Cantonese, the word *wonton* is written as "cloud-swallowing", while the Mandarin term *huntun* means "chaos", referring to the primordial state before the separation of Heaven and Earth.

During the Tang Dynasty, the world of *bing* underwent a lexicological division. Fried, baked, or steamed breads and boiled dumplings remained *bing*, but noodles became *mian*. Lacking the hard durum wheat of Western Asia, the Chinese concentrated on making fresh noodles for eating immediately rather than dried noodles for storage. These included *mian* made from rolling dough into ropes, cutting sheets of it into strips, or pushing very soft dough through the holes of a sieve into boiling water. Over the century or two that followed, *mian* grew in importance from a beloved snack into the full-fledged basis of northern Chinese meals (Coe, 2009: 89-90).

In the Yuan Dynasty, the government supported foreign trade and welcomed foreign religious teachers of many faiths. Missionaries and traders traveled back and forth between China and areas in the west, bringing to China new ideas, foods, and medicines. Best known of the foreigners believed to have reached China during this period was the Venetian merchant Marco Polo, whose account of his travels portrays the wealth and splendor of Chinese cities. Interest in China and Chinese people and things resulted in a large body of writing by Europeans. This interest has waxed and waned, never fading completely.

3.3.2 The 16th to the 18th Century

Early massive contact between China and the West occurred at the early 16th century when the activities of navigators, travelers and missionaries were at their peak. To preserve the government's monopoly on foreign contacts, the rules of the Ming Dynasty prohibited unauthorized dealings between Chinese and foreigners. These prohibitions were unpopular and unenforceable, and from about the mid-15th century, the Chinese readily collaborated with foreign traders in widespread smuggling. By 1557, the Portuguese had taken control of Macao, a small trading station on China's coast. Soon, the Spanish also were trading illegally along the coast. Representatives of the Dutch East India Company, after unsuccessfully trying to capture Macao from the Portuguese, took control of coastal Taiwan in 1624 and began developing trade contacts on the mainland in nearby Fujian and Zhejiang provinces. In 1637, a squadron of five English ships shot its way into Guangzhou and disposed of its cargoes there. Christian missionaries followed the traders. Jesuits, members of a Roman

Catholic religious order, showed respect for Chinese culture and overcame the foreigners' reputation for lawlessness. The Jesuits were an important bond between the East and the West. By the latter part of the 17th century they held first place as authorities on China. They usually gave favorable reports of the Chinese. The most eminent of the Jesuit missionaries was Matteo Ricci, who acquired a substantial knowledge of the Chinese language and of Confucian learning. During the latter part of the Ming dynasty, the Jesuits established communities in many cities of south and central China and built a church in Beijing under imperial patronage. Jesuits even served as astronomers in the Ming court. Some officials and members of the court became Jesuit converts or sympathizers, and European books on scientific subjects and Christian theology were published in Chinese.

The stories brought back by travelers and traders made China and things Chinese the subject of fascination to English-speaking people, and their interest grew to a height in the late 17th and the 18th centuries (Chan & Kwok, 1985: 3). Some borrowings naming the new imports and relating directly to their seafaring commercial activities did indeed come into the English language. *Tea* was becoming more and more popular as a beverage. The bulk of the cargo of the East India Company was tea (Chan & Kwok, 1985: 4). With tea came porcelain ware—*china*, also brought by the ships of the East India Company. The vogue of hoarding porcelain started in the late 17th century. Also imported from China and much coveted were paintings, wall paper, lacquered ware and objects d'art.

The early spellings of *tea* include *tay*, *thea*, *tey* or *chaa* and *cha* in 1590s. The distribution of the different forms of the word in Europe reflects the spread of use of the beverage. The modern English form, along with French *thé*, Spanish *te*, German *Tee*, etc., derive via Dutch *thee* from the Amoy form, reflecting the role of the Dutch as the chief importers of the leaves (through the Dutch East India Company, from 1610). Meanwhile, Russian *chai*, Persian *cha*, Greek *tsai*, Arabic *shay*, and Turkish *çay* all came overland from the Mandarin form. *Bohea* (a kind of black tea, taking its name from Chinese *Wu-i*, name of district), together with the names of some other teas, appeared in writings of the period.

It was only during the 18th century that regular commercial interactions between the English and the Chinese were established. It was this contact situation that saw the emergence of Chinese pidgin English, a trade language which is a mixture of European languages combined with words of Cantonese and Mandarin origin. The English traders were at the mercy of those Chinese who professed to have a sufficient knowledge of some foreign language as to enable them to act as interpreters. This class, known as the "linguists", conducted all the trading negotiations between the Chinese and foreigners by means of pidgin English. Indeed the word *pidgin* is itself a "corrupted" form of the English word "business". Chinese pidgin English consisted of a small vocabulary made up of words derived mainly from English and Portuguese, but including Malay and Hindi words, and rules of syntax based on Chinese.

*Chop* and *chow* are among the words that are said to be pidgin in origin. The etymology of these words is not known. Each has a number of different meanings. *Chop-chop* means "quickly, at once". The word *chopstick* comes from pidgin English *chop* "quick" + "sticks", an attempt to translate the meaning shown by the Chinese 筷子. A *chophouse is a Chinese custom-house*. *Chop* can also mean "quality, grade, or brand", so that *first chop* means "first rate". It can also refer to the hulk of a boat remodeled and anchored for storage or residence, and a *chop boat* in China is a "licensed lighter for carrying passengers or freight". *Chow-chow* in pidgin English means "mixed, assorted", as *chowchow sweetmeats*.

*Kowtow*, the Chinese custom of touching the ground with the forehead, literally means "knock the head". The word first became current through the literature of travelers to China from England in the late 18th and early 19th centuries. "Otto Jespersen, in *The Growth and Structure of the English Language*, giving examples of English words borrowed from various sources, writes, 'From Chinese we have kowtow'" (Chan, 1983: 62). In 1793, the Great Britain dispatched to China an embassy headed by Lord Macartney. Although Macartney refused to perform the ceremonial "kowtow", the embassy was received by the Qianlong Emperor at his summer residence at Rehe. However, Macartney's requests, which included the opening of additional ports to foreign trade and the accreditation of an ambassador to the Chinese court, were politely but categorically refused (Roberts, 2002).

*Kowtow* is Chinese culture-specific, and in different context, it can be an expression of respect, submission, gratitude, or worship. In the *Longman Dictionary of Contemporary English*, *kowtow* is defined as an intransitive verb, meaning "to be too eager to obey or be polite to someone in authority". For example, "We will not kowtow to the government." In the *Collins English Dictionary*, two senses of *kowtow* are listed: 1. to touch the forehead to the ground as a sign of deference: a former Chinese custom; 2. (often followed by *to*) to be servile or obsequious (towards). The word *kowtow* is often seen in the translated versions of Chinese ancient literary works. Here is an excerpt from *The Dream of Red Mansion* translated by David Hawkes.

> Jia Zheng rose from his seat and kowtowed in the appropriate direction for this act of Imperial clemency. He also bowed to the aide to express his profound gratitude for the prince's intervention on his behalf. "Be so good as to convey my thanks to His Highness. Tomorrow I shall attend court in order to express my gratitude to His Majesty in person, and shall also present myself at His Highness's palace to make my kowtow."

### 3.3.3 The 19th to the beginning of 20th century

Few westerners had penetrated the Chinese interior since the days of Marco Polo. Catholic missionaries, merchants and others with commercial interests arrived in China early in large numbers in the 19th century. Under the Treaty of Nanjing which concluded the First Opium War (1839-1842), five Chinese ports (Guangzhou, Xiamen, Fuzhou, Ningbo and Shanghai) were opened for trade and residence to British merchants, a right which was soon extended to other Western nations. In these treaty ports Western communities were established. Most of them were officials, merchants and missionaries. Their residence in China was of varying duration. They had become acquainted with and given some currency to Chinese names associated with daily life. China and Chinese themes appeared frequently in their writings.

The Qing rulers, overall, remained hostile to the foreign presence within China and the ordinary population showed little enthusiasm for the arrival of foreigners. The Chinese called the strangers barbarians and seemed to loathe them as real demons and inferior spirits. A few have been in existence for a long time, e. g. *foreign devil*. *Foreign devil* is a loan translation for the Chinese name for foreigners 番鬼. The premodifier has been softened in that its literal translation would be "barbarian", rather than just "foreign". The loan translation has a synonym in *fanqui*, later *gweilo*, which subsequently replaced both in popularity (Chan & Kwok, 1985: 59).

*Cumshaw* is a term of uncertain etymology, although all standard dictionaries like the OED. and Webster state that it is of Chinese origin. Webster defines it as "present, gratuity; also bribe, payoff". It was probably British Navy personnel who first picked up *cumshaw* in Chinese ports, during the First Opium War of 1839. *Cumshaw* is from a word that means "grateful thanks" in the dialect of Xiamen, a port in southeast China. Apparently, sailors heard it from the beggars who hung around the ports, and mistook it as the word for a handout. Since then, U. S. sailors have given *cumshaw* its own unique application, for something obtained through unofficial means. Outside of naval circles, meanings of *cumshaw* range from a harmless gratuity or gift to bending the rules a little to outright bribery. There is another interpretation of its origins, that is, *cumshaw* is pidgin English and is a perversion of "Come ashore", the cry uttered by those soliciting money from the sailors in Chinese ports from the early days of trading. In today's English, it usually refers to a relatively small amount of money given for services rendered (as by a waiter).

In the 19th century, not only was contact brought about by westerners coming to China, but Chinese immigrants began in the middle of the century to bring their language with them to the United States, Canada, Australasia and some South-East Asian countries. And this sort of language contact resulted in borrowings of words, largely those naming aspects of Chinese way of life.

The game of *mahjong* has been known to the Westerner since the Treaty Port days (Chan & Kwok, 1985: 194). The name *mahjong* (or *mahjongg*) was adopted as a phonetic loan with the game, played usually by four persons. There are 144 domino-like pieces used in playing this game; in the past these pieces were often made of ivory. Today they are more often plastic. In the past centuries *mahjong* was introduced to Japan, America and other countries, where rules are modified. *Mahjong* was discouraged in 1950s-1960s because of its association with a decadent life. Now it is a common means of household entertainment and a competitive athletic sport as well. The term *mahjong* is recorded in almost every mainstream English dictionary.

*Chase the dragon* is a slang word by drug users, meaning "to take heroin (or heroin mixed with another smokable drug) by heating it on a piece of folded tin foil and inhaling the fumes". The phrase is reputed to be translated from Chinese and apparently arises from the fact that the fumes move up and down the piece of tin foil with the movements of the molten heroin powder, and these undulating movements resemble the tail of the dragon in Chinese myths. This exotic aspect of the expression enhances its picturesque quality.

The picturesque quality of some translation loans may appeal to the imagination. For example, tiny bound feet were considered by some to be a sign of beauty in the Qing Dynasty and went by the rather romantic name of 三寸金莲, literally "three-inch golden lilies". The English translation, sometimes shortened to *golden lilies*, can be found in various publications about the practice of foot-binding during the period.

During the latter half of the 19th century the Qing empire was in decline. The United States was developing industries, and frontier regions needed cheap labor. Industrialization and colonial expansion by Western European nations created similar needs which the impoverished Chinese immigrants could fulfill. The California Gold Rush (1848-1855) attracted some tens of thousands people from Latin America, Europe, Australia, and China. From 1850 until 1882, more than 322,000 Chinese entered the United States. Some were merchants and craftsmen, but most were unskilled laborers and peasants from rural areas of Guangdong and Fujian. The vast majority were Cantonese speakers, a number spoke Hakka, and those from certain areas of the Chaoshan district spoke variants of the Southern Min dialect.

There are two terms relating to illegal immigrants, i. e. *snake boat* and *snake head*, meaning respectively a boat carrying illegal immigrants and a person in charge of such an illegal operation. The metaphor is picturesque and imaginative, the slithering slimy character of the snake suggesting the deviousness of the perpetrators and the circuitous nature of the route that has usually to be taken.

Chinese migration was a transnational flow of people, social networks, and cultural values. Chinese immigrants arrived in America with their own lifestyles, labor and vocational skills, business expertise and capital, family rituals and traditions, religious and philosophical beliefs. Food is one of the earliest and probably the most visible aspects of transnational Chinese culture in America. Canton Restaurant, with seating for three hundred, was established in San Francisco as early as

1849. A business directory in 1856 lists five restaurants and thirty eight grocery stores among eighty eight Chinese businesses in San Francisco (Liu, 2009).

Out of the array of dishes the Americans preferred, *chop suey* stood out as their favorite. *Chop suey* is more accurately transcribed as *za sui* (Mandarin) or *shap sui* (Cantonese). *Shap* means mixed or blended together; *sui* means bits or small fragments. Read together, the most common translation is "odds and ends." As a culinary term, it refers to a hodgepodge stew of many different ingredients. It is a preparation of sliced pork or chicken cooked with bean sprouts, onions, celery, bamboo shoots, and water chestnuts until everything is mushy and flavorless, then served with a gummy, translucent sauce over white rice. *Chop suey* was described as the staple food of the New York Chinese and even the "national dish of China" (Coe, 2009: 261). One account claims that it was invented by Chinese American cooks working on the transcontinental railroad in the 19th century. Another tale is that it was created during the Qing Dynasty premier Li Hongzhang's visit to the United States in 1896 by his chef, who tried to create a meal suitable for both Chinese and American palates. Another story is that Li wandered to a local Chinese restaurant after the hotel kitchen had closed, where the chef, embarrassed that he had nothing ready to offer, came up with the new dish using scraps of leftovers. Yet no evidence has been found to support the story that Li Hongzhang ate *chop suey* in the United States. Up and down the East Coast, *chop suey* spreaded to all the big cities and many of the larger towns. *Chop suey* had become emblematic of Chinese food in many American people's eyes. From 1900 to the 1960s, most Chinese restaurants in America were called *Chop Suey Houses*, and *chop suey* was synonymous with Chinese food in the United States. From American English, the term gained currency in other forms of English.

Another loan which found its way into American English at around the same time as *chop suey* is *chow mein*. The word means "fried noodles", *chow* meaning "fried" and *mein* meaning "noodles". The pronunciation *chow mein* is an English corruption of the Taishanese pronunciation. The Taishan dialect is one variety of Contonese.

The companion loan, *chow fan* ("fried rice"), however, enjoys a rather lower level of currency. Unlike *chow mein*, it is not included in any standard dictionary of either American or British English. The disparity in currency between the seemingly related terms appears to have arisen because of the disparity in the degree of familiarity with the respective things referred to. Americans in the Gold Rush days took to the crispy noodles of the *chow mein* dish. By analogy, when fried rice became more popular *chow fan* started to gain currency but has not yet reached the same level of familiarity as *chow mein*.

By the late 1940s, there were about 4,300 Chinese restaurants in the continental United States, and 7 percent of the American population frequented Chinese restaurants. Ten years later the number of Chinese restaurants grew to 4,500 but, even more remarkably, they had over 20 percent of Americans as their frequent customers. In 1959, New York City alone had about 750 Chinese restaurants. Food related words have become widely known during the booming of Chinese food.

The Chinese migrants established certain societies based on locality or kinship, with elaborate structures, and names like *Hui guan* and *fang* to denote the levels of organization. These terms evidently never caught on beyond the Chinese-speaking community. The conduct of the migrants was conditioned by Confucianism, and their beliefs were influenced by Taoist as well as Buddhist philosophy. The terms Confucian, Confucianism, Taoist and Taoism gained somewhat greater immediacy (Chan & Kwok, 1985: 17). Confucianism is sometimes termed a religion, but it is really more of an ethical system, or system of norms. In its all-pervasiveness and its flexibility and adaptability to circumstances, it is somewhat analogous to the role of Judaeo-Christian norms in Western societies, where even those who dispute or reject those norms still find themselves shaped by them, consciously or not (Mitter, 2008: 7).

Compared to the Chinese in the United States, the Chinese in Britain appear to have made relatively little impact, linguistic or otherwise. The main source of contact for the Chinese immigrants with the English would be through the food they serve in the growing number of Chinese restaurants and take-aways (Chan & Kwok, 1985: 14). It would seem that Chinese loan words, whether in the form of phonetic loans or loan translations, have tended to enter the English vocabulary more through books, the media and returning expatriates rather than through direct contact between the Chinese and the British in Britain. The same sort of situation appears in Australia. The direct contact between the Chinese immigrants and the Australians appears not to have resulted in lexical borrowings which are distinctive of Australian English (Chan & Kwok, 1985: 15).

In Hong Kong, from the mid-nineteenth century Chinese and English have existed side by side, resulting in mutual lexical borrowing. Though the borrowing from Chinese to date has not been very significant, it is evident that, because of the cosmopolitan nature of Hong Kong and the easy movement of people to and from Hong Kong, some of the lexical innovations may find their way outside Hong Kong, gain international currency and eventual inclusion in standard English dictionaries (Chan & Kwok, 1985: vii).

The latter part of the 19th century and the beginning of the 20th saw an increase in proficiency in English on the part of the Chinese-speaker, and Chinese pidgin English as a distinct language system ceased to exist. A few words from pidgin have survived. Some of these are specifically designated as being pidgin in origin in various dictionaries. It was merely after the second half of the 19th century that great numbers of Chinese loanwords were introduced into the English lexicon.

During the World War II, western countries showed more concern with Chinese battlefield. The phonetic loan *Kuomintang*, the Chinese Nationalist Party, became part of the vocabulary of the American cognoscenti, while the Chinese Communist Party went by its translation form (Chan & Kwok, 1985: 19).

*Gung ho*, meaning "wholeheartedly enthusiastic", is used mostly in American English as an adjective. The term was first popularized when the unit of the U. S. Marines that served under General Evans F. Carlson in World War II adopted the expression in its slogan. According to the *Collins English Dictionary*, "If you say that someone is gung ho, you mean that they are very enthusiastic or eager to do something, for example to fight in a battle." The term may well be pidgin English since the expression 工合 does not in fact occur in Chinese. The English expression *gung ho* is not widely known to the

Chinese people, and English speakers rarely know details of its etymology. From its early associations with militaristic or patriotic ardor, *gung ho* has become extended in use to other areas. The following are some examples from the news media.

> O'Donnell wrongly equates women's instinct to protect their health and lives with selfishness (instead of self-defense), and unfairly, utterly ignores far more violent selfish tendencies in men. It is pretty hypocritical of a party that is so gung ho on guns, aggression, war, capital punishment and polarizing hate language (and so silent on the male role in domestic violence, child abuse and sexual assault) to co-opt "family values", and accuse feminists and abortion of causing all violence in society. (San Francisco Chronicle, 1996/06/20)

> I am not willing to sit back and wait for something much worse than a Sept. 11 to occur before our government decides to take action. Maybe if our last administration had taken strong action, things might have turned out differently. The things that President Bush is dealing with today are a direct result of a lack of action for eight years. I have a question for George Bush: If you had two 20-year-old sons instead of daughters, would you be so gung ho about a war with Iraq? With the coming elections so near, I think President Bush sees Iraq and Saddam Hussein as weapons of mass distraction. (Chicago Sun-Times, 2002/10/14)

American soldiers who were fighting in Chinese battlefield needed to know some cultural background of China. For example, in *A Pocket Guide to China*, a small booklet dispatched to them, *face* is explained as follows:

> Chinese people consider it important not to hurt anyone's feelings and they will appreciate consideration of their own feelings. This is sometimes called *face*, which simply means self-respect. There is about as much of it in one country as another, but the Chinese pay more attention to preserving it than we do. They do not criticize each other as frankly as we do, and there are certain rules of courtesy, particularly to the old, from the young. Old people in China are highly

respected, even revered, and their advice valued. Lack of respect to the old is therefore a sign of bad manners. (U. S. Government Printing Office, 1942: 9)

### 3.3.4 After 1949

Great social and cultural changes have taken place after the founding of the People's Republic of China. Some words in the field of politics, economy and other realms of thought in China are transmitted through mainstream Western news media to a larger audience. Some key words have become marks of certain important social events.

The term *paper tiger* indicated the hostilities existed between the United States and the new republic. It is a direct translation from the ancient Chinese proverb, first received public attention in 1946 when Mao Zedong accused the U. S. of being a *paper tiger*. Although now applied in widely varying contexts, *paper tiger* remains an effective political invective and the currency of the borrowed phrase is fairly wide (Chan & Kwok, 1985: 23). A similar case is the *running dog*, which means an unprincipled person who helps or flatters those more powerful and often evil.

After the opening up policy was adopted in 1980s, China began to have a wider range of commercial, technical, governmental, and institutional contacts with Western countries. The overseas Chinese have always been an important part of the story of China's development. Meanwhile, China has strived to accelerate the country's modernization by sending students abroad not in their hundreds, but tens of thousands, to study science and technology. With the rapid exchanges with the outside world, more and more words are translated literally into English to introduce new concepts and new phenomena in China, such *as Four Modernizations*, *women hold up half the sky*, *work unit*, *seek truth from facts*, *reform and opening-up*, *one-child policy*, *iron rice bowl*, *breaking one's rice bowl*, *special economic zone*, *one country with two systems*, *all-round education*, *township enterprise*, *state treasury bond*, *joint ventures*, *laid-off workers*, *export-oriented economy*, *moderately well-off society*, *socialist market economy*, *socialist spiritual civilization*, *the Three Represents*, *peaceful rising*, etc.

The method of loan translation is effective in dealing with many terms coined by the Chinese to cover the important events and concepts. Take the *one-child policy* for example. It refers to a part of the family planning policy, which was introduced in 1979 to curb a then-surging population and limit the demands for water and other resources as well as to alleviate social, economic and environmental problems in China. It began to be formally phased out in 2015. *Project Hope* is a broad-based educational charity initiated and organized by the China Youth Development Foundation (CYDF). In accordance with government guidelines for raising money for education, its main purpose is to raise money from all sectors of society to fund a Project Hope Foundation whereby students otherwise too poor to attend or remain in school can do so, and the physical conditions of their education can be improved. The foundation focuses on remote and poor areas, especially in western China. Its goal is to improve the standards and conditions of elementary education in those areas and to help all students stay in school, thereby also fulfilling the government policy of Nine Years' Compulsory Education. Since 1989, the foundation has helped 23 million students enter or return to school, and about 8,000 Hope Schools have been built. The term *holiday economy* appeared on the background that the Chinese government lengthened the National Day holiday to a week on 10 October 1999 and did the same to the International Labor Day on 1 May 2000. The move was designed to encourage the Chinese to spend their bank savings so as to boost the economy. As a result, the country is experiencing waves of travel mania each year. While tourism-related businesses have reaped profits, problems like traffic congestion, overbooking and overcrowding do increase.

With the booming of its economy, China has become a world power and what is happening in China is increasingly attracting the world's attention. As a result, more and more new words are created or translated to describe the changes in China. These words are distinctive features of the China English.

## 3.4 Transmission Languages for Chinese Loanwords in English

Language borrowing may be direct or indirect, depending upon the ways of contact. In direct borrowing, elements of Language A are borrowed into Language B directly. This is the commonest way of borrowing. In some cases, the elements of Language A come into Language B through Language C, or through Language C then into Language D... then into Language B. This is indirect borrowing. The history of a loanword in English might be complex because it has often passed through a series of languages before reaching English. The ultimate origin of a word is not always the source whence it has penetrated into English (Jespersen, 1922).

The word *chess* is an example. It was borrowed in the 14th century from Middle French *esches*. The French word had been, in turn, borrowed from Medieval Latin, which got it from Arabic, which had borrowed it from Persian *shah* ("king"). The direct or immediate source of chess is Middle French, but its ultimate source (as far back as we can trace its history) is Persian.

Loanwords have, as it were, a life of their own that cuts across the boundaries between languages (Algeo, 2010: 248). Some languages had made contributions of various degrees to the spreading of Chinese words, including Portuguese, Japanese, etc.

Before 1637 when British commercial ships came to China for the tea business, the import of Chinese words was mainly via other channels. In the 16th century, Portuguese merchants brought tea to Europe. The word *cha* entered English vocabulary and the word *tea* was introduced by Dutch in 1602. After 1637, English language and Chinese language had the direct contact, so that more and more Chinese words were known and adopted by English speakers. A *comprador* (买办, literally "to buy and to do tasks") was a personage peculiar to the China Coast, who represented the *taipan* in all his dealings with Chinese traders (Chan & Kwok, 1985: 204). The term *comprador* is a Portuguese word that means "buyer", and it derives from the Latin *comparare*, which means "to procure". The original usage of the word in East Asia meant a native servant in European households in Guangzhou in southern China or the neighboring Portuguese colony at Macao who went to market to barter their employers' wares. The term then evolved to mean the native contract suppliers who worked for foreign companies in East Asia or the native managers of firms in East Asia. *Compradors* held important positions in southern China buying and selling tea, silk, cotton and yarn for foreign corporations and working in foreign-owned banks.

*Horde* in English is the transliteration of "鄂尔多斯" (Zhang, 2014). "鄂尔多斯" is originally a word in Mongol, meaning "mobile camp, mobile palace". When the Mongol military troops invaded Europe, the word entered Turkish language as "ordu" and then Polish as "horda", meaning royal camp. The word later was borrowed into French and German. In the 16th century it finally found its place in English with the form of "horde". The meaning changed into "a group of nomads, especially of a people who live by hunting and foraging for food".

In ancient times, China was East Asia's dominant civilization. Other societies—notably the Japanese, Koreans, and Vietnamese—were strongly influenced by China, adopting features of Chinese art, food, material culture, philosophy, government, technology, and written language. China and Japan have a long history of contact. Cultural exchange between China and Japan reached its peak during the Tang Dynasty. Kyoto, the beautiful ancient capital of Japan, was even built according to the design of Chang'an (now Xi'an), the capital of China during the Tang Dynasty. The Japanese also adopted many aspects of Chinese life style. Thus, for example, cultural characteristics that are associated only with Japan today—from the highly ceremonious, meditative Tea Ceremony to household items such as tatami (the matted floor for sitting and sleeping)—had their origins in ancient China. The historical contacts with China have left strong marks in the Japanese lexicon. Roughly 60 percent of the Japanese vocabulary consists of loanwords of Chinese origin, a figure comparable to the proportion of Latinate words in the English vocabulary (Shibatani, 2009). English played a significant role in the transformation of Japan from a feudal, closed country to a modern nation. As a result, English loanwords are pervasively used regardless of domains, registers, and socio-economic groups in Japan today. It is estimated that 5 percent of the vocabulary items used in daily Japanese conversation and 11 percent of the total words produced in conversation are from English (Hoffer, 2005). On the other hand, because of its own distinctive social and administrative systems and cultures, Japan has contributed quite a large number of loanwords to the English language (Doi, 2014). Some words are simple transliterations of Japanese language words for concepts inherent to Japanese culture, but some are actually words of Chinese origin that were first exposed to English via Japan. Moody (1996: 408) lists several languages that contributed to the spreading of Chinese terms in the English language. Among these transmission languages, Japanese has the largest number of words.

One typical example is the term *tycoon*, which has entered the English language via Japanese. *Tycoon* is so generally known that it is inevitably unmarked and unglossed when it appears in its written form. The use of it by F. Scott Fitzgerald in the title of his novel, *The Last Tycoon*, seems to suggest the word has been totally assimilated into the English lexicon. It is recorded in OED. as well as Webster, Collins and Random House. The etymology given in OED indicates that *tycoon* came via Japanese *taikun* "great lord" or "prince" and is ultimately from Chinese. The two Chinese morphemes are 大 meaning "great" and 官 which refers to a high ranking official. From the political sphere the word in its transliterated form has moved to the commercial, where it now refers to "a businessman having great wealth and power" (Chan & Kwok, 1985: 109).

Among the words relating to Chinese religion and philosophy, one of the best known is *Chan* (better known in the West by its Japanese name, *Zen*), referring to a form of Buddhism introduced into China in the 6th century. In the Tang times, Buddhism fully penetrated Chinese daily life. Among the educated elite, *Chan* gained popularity. *Chan* teachings rejected the authority of the sutra writings as the words of the Buddha and claimed the superiority of mind-to-mind transmission of Buddhist truth. According to *Chan* Buddhism, enlightenment could be achieved suddenly through insight into one's own true nature. The emphasis for the disciples of *Chan* is put on enlightenment by the most direct possible means. Formal studies and observances are acceptable only when they formed part of such means. *Chan* Buddhism was introduced into Japan as early as the 7th century but flowered only in the 12th and the 13th centuries. By the mid-20th century, *Zen* had become one of the best-known of the Buddhist schools in the Western world (Kuiper, 2011: 142). The word *Zen* came into English via Japanese and gained a certain amount of publicity from its association with the hippy movement of the 1960s. Random House gives a pronunciation based on Putonghua: *ch'an* (Chan & Kwok, 1985: 168).

*The Browser's Dictionary of Foreign Words and Phrases* (2001) included some Japanese loanwords which were originally from Chinese.

**bento**, **obento** [Japanese, from Chinese]: A complete meal served in a lacquered box divided into sections that keep the various dishes apart.

**bonze** [Japanese, from Chinese]: A Japanese Buddhist monk.

**daikon** [Japanese, from Chinese: big root]: In Asian cooking, a long, white, winter radish used raw (grated or shredded), or pickled.

**daimyo**, **daimio** [Japanese, from Chinese: great name]: Formerly, a title given to the hereditary feudal lords of Japan.

**dan** [Japanese, from Chinese: grade]: In the martial arts, the highest ranks of proficiency in judo, karate, etc., symbolized by the wearing of a black cloth belt.

**daruma** [Japanese, from a Chinese transliteration of the Sanskrit: dharma]: A large Japanese doll made in the image of a seated Buddhist monk, a symbol of the Indian monk Bodhidharma, who founded the Zen sect of Buddhism; it is thought to be a good-luck charm.

**futon** [Japanese, from Chinese]: A traditional Japanese mattress, made of heavy cotton and stuffed with layers of batting, that can be folded and put away when not in use; usually placed on the floor for sleeping.

**geisha** [Japanese, from Chinese: arts person]: A Japanese woman, trained in the arts of music, dance, and conversation, who acts as a professional hostess and companion for men.

**go** [Japanese, from Chinese]: A Japanese strategy game similar to chess, played by two people on a checkered board (goban) with 361 intersections; players attempt to conquer territory by surrounding vacant points with boundaries made of their own "stones" or pieces.

**hibachi** [Japanese, from Chinese]: A Japanese style brazier, covered with a grill, that holds burning charcoal for outdoor cooking or heating.

**honcho** [Japanese, from Chinese]: In slang, a chief, boss, or assertive leader.

**judo** [Japanese, from Chinese: gentle way]: A method of weaponless combat based on jujitsu, designed to overpower an opponent without inflicting serious harm. The sport of judo forbids the use of dangerous moves and requires great courtesy in practice.

**jujitsu**, **jiujitsu** [Japanese, from Chinese: soft technique]: A system of hand-to-hand combat that developed in the 1500s, involving methods of kicking, hitting, throwing, etc., calculated to turn an opponent's weight and strength against him. Judo, karate, and aikido are based partly on principles of jujitsu.

**kendo** [Japanese, from Chinese: way of the sword]: A Japanese style of fencing with flexible bamboo swords, practiced largely among student, police, and military organizations. Contestants wear protective clothing and head guards.

**koan** [Japanese, from Chinese: public notice]: In Japanese Zen Buddhism, a meditation discipline for students consisting of paradoxical statements or questions that pose mental dilemmas for which an answer is demanded.

**kyogen** [Japanese, from Chinese]: In Japanese theater, a short comic interlude performed between the plays of a no cycle, to ease the tension of the drama. Kyogen are very broad in their humor, last about twenty minutes, and do not use music.

**ninja** [Japanese, from Chinese: he who endures]: In feudal Japan, a mercenary skilled in the martial arts and in covert operations such as espionage, sabotage, and assassination.

**No, Noh** [Japanese, from Chinese: ability]: An aristocratic and highly stylized form of drama, developed in Japan in the 14th century, using poetry, prose, chorus, and dance. No plays are short, tragic, and have little plot.

**shiatsu** [Japanese, from Chinese]: A Japanese form of massage that includes the use of acupuncture.

**shogun** [Japanese, from Chinese: lead the army]: Originally, the title given to military commanders in Japan from the 8th through the 12th centuries. From then until 1868, the shogun (whose office was hereditary) was the actual ruler of Japan, under whom the emperor was a figurehead.

**sumie** [Japanese]: A style of monochromatic ink painting, brought from China in the mid-1300s by Zen Buddhists.

**tofu** [Japanese, from Chinese]: In oriental cooking, a white, mild-flavored curd made from soybean milk, also called bean curd.

**waka** [Japanese, from Chinese]: A native Japanese verse form, one distinct from poetry written in other languages, or from verse written in Chinese by a Japanese poet.

**zori** [Japanese, from Chinese]: A Japanese straw or rubber sandal with a flat sole and a thong between the first and second toes.

## 3.5 Summary

From the above survey of the Chinese loanwords in the English language, it is safe to say that the vocabulary of English shows considerable Chinese influence. However, once we move to individual word histories, we are typically dealing in probabilities rather than certainties: in some cases we cannot be entirely certain that any Chinese influence occurred; in some others, we can be reasonably certain that there was some kind of influence, but the exact mechanism is uncertain. For many of the word histories, it is no easy matter to pin down precisely when borrowing occurred, and in which social and cultural conditions.

Because of the disparate nature of the Chinese and English languages and essentially of the two cultures, it is probably unlikely that the English language will, as it did Latin and Greek and Romance words during the Renaissance, embark on large-scale importation of Chinese words into the English vocabulary. Soame Jenyns wrote in 1935 in the Introduction to his *A Background to Chinese Painting*, "China is still distant enough from our lands to be invested with the glamour of an undiscovered country. The manners of the Chinese, their methods of life, their ways and their politics, their art have an engaging quality; yet they are so far remote from our own habits of thought and life as to make it difficult for us to appreciate the problems of their society." (Chan & Kwok, 1985: 217) But developments on the international scene and the increased contacts with China on the individual, institutional and national levels seem to ensure that the language of the largest number of people in the world will lose its sense of total remoteness and total strangeness to the English speaking world.

# Chapter 4 Chinese Loanwords in English Dictionaries

## 4.1 Introduction

The vocabulary of English is not an unchanging list of words. How large is English vocabulary? It is a question to which no clear answer can be given. The blurbs on the jackets of various dictionaries may state that the dictionary contains "more than" 200,000 words, but that is difficult to determine. All one can count is "entries" or "headwords", and even that turns out to be a slippery notion because what is a headword in one dictionary may be subordinated—listed below the main entry—in another (Stockwell & Minkova, 2001: 178). Over 600,000 items are included in the OED, which, however, does not list specialist scientific and technical terminology.

Loanwords make up a huge proportion of the words in any large dictionary of English (Durkin, 2014: 4). John Algeo (2010: 248) suggests that "an overwhelming majority of the words in any large dictionary, as well as many we use everyday, either came from other languages or were coined from elements of foreign words. So the foreign component in our word stock is of great importance".

In the following sections we will examine the words of Chinese origins in English dictionaries.

## 4.2 Chinese Loanwords in English Dictionaries of Foreign Terms

Dictionaries can be classified into different types on the basis of several criteria. Dictionaries of borrowed words (foreign words), as one category of special dictionaries, record words that are borrowed into the language from time to time. These dictionaries, in a limited sense, come under the class of etymological dictionaries. Words from other cultures usually will first appear in such dictionaries as the first step of their institutionalization.

We have surveyed five English dictionaries of foreign words and expressions to see how they treat Chinese loanwords respectively. It is clear that the number of Chinese words varies, even though there exists some overlapping. The details are illustrated in Table 4.1.

**Table 4.1 Chinese loanwords in Fiver English Dictionaries of Foreign Words**

| Dictionaries | Chinese loanwords |
|---|---|
| *A Dictionary of Foreign Words and Phrases in Current English* (1966) | *sampan*, *typhoon*, *kowtow*, *loquat*, *cheong-sam*, *kuomintang* |
| *A Concise Dictionary of Foreign Expressions* (1982) | *char*, *chin-chin*, *chow mein*, *kowtow*, *mah-jong*, *sampan*, *shantung*, *taipan* |

| Dictionaries | Chinese loanwords |
|---|---|
| *The Harper Dictionary of Foreign Terms* (3rd edition, 1987) | *cha*, *chop suey*, *chow*, *chow fan*, *chow mein*, *cumshaw*, *dim sum*, *ding hao*, *gung ho*, *kang*, *kan pei*, *kiang*(*jiang*), *kowtow*, *kun*, *kung fu*, *mahjong*, *mao tai*, *sampan*, *tai chi chuan*, *tao*, *wan sui*, *yamen* (*yamun*) |
| *The Oxford Dictionary of Foreign Words and Phrases* (1997) | *ginseng*, *li*, *sampan*, *yang*, *yin*, *feng-shui*, *hong*, *pe-tsai*, *souchong*, *t'ai chi*, *chopsuey*, *chow mein*, *k'ai shu*, *kowtow*, *kung fu*, *kylin*, *Lohan*, *nien hao*, *pak-choi*, *san-hsien*, *taipan*, *t'ing*, *te*, *ti-tzu*, *tong*, *wei ch'i*, *yang ch'in*, *yueh ch'in*, *an-hua*, *cheongsam*, *dazibo*, *dim sum*, *erh hu*, *fu yung*, *ganbei*, *gung-ho*, *hoisin*, *ko*, *kuei*, *kwai-lo*, *lei*, *ling chih*, *mah-jong*, *mee*, *mei ping*, *pai-hua*, *pakapoo*, *p'an*, *putonghua*, *qinghaosu*, *samfu*, *san ts'ai*, *subgum*, *tu-mo*, *ve-tsin*, *wen jen*, *wen-yen*, *wok*, *wonton*, *wushu*, *wu ts'ai*, *ying ch'ing*, *yuan* |
| *The Facts on File Dictionary of Foreign Words and Phrases* (2nd edition, 2008) | *bok choy*, *cheongsam*, *chop suey*, *chow mein*, *dim sum*, *feng-shui*, *fu yung*, *ginseng*, *gung-ho*, *kaolin*, *kowtow*, *kung fu*, *mahjong*, *mandarin*, *qigong* (*chi kung*), *sampan*, *shih-tzu*, *tai chi*, *tao*, *wok*, *wonton*, *yang*, *yin* |

These five dictionaries, which belong to the small scale ones, have different inclusion of Chinese loanwords. Words collected in all the five dictionaries are *sampan*, *kowtow*. In four of the five dictionaries, we can find *chow mein*. *Cheongsam*, *mah-jong*, *shantung*, *chop suey*, *gung ho*, *kung fu*, *tai chi* (*tai chi chuan*, *t'ai chi*), *bok choy* (*pak-choi*, *pe-tsai*), *dim sum* occur in three dictionaries. *Char* (*cha*), *mah-jong*, *tao*, *feng-shui*, *fu yung*, *ginseng*, *taipan*, *wok*, *yin*, *yang*, *kan pei* (*ganbei*) occur in two dictionaries. The rest just occur in one of the five dictionaries, including *typhoon*, *loquat*, *kuomintang*, *chin-chin*, *chow*, *chow fan*, *cumshaw*, *ding hao*, *kang*, *kiang* (*jiang*), *kun*, *maotai*, *wan sui*, *yamen* (*yamun*), *fu yung*, *kaolin*, *mandarin*, *qigong* (*chi kung*), *shih-tzu*, *wonton*, *li*, *hong*, *souchong*, *k'ai shu*, *kylin*, *lohan*, *nien hao*, *san-hsien*, *t'ing*, *te*, *ti-tzu*, *tong*, *wei ch'i*, *yang ch'in*, *yueh ch'in*, *an-hua*, *dazibao*, *erh hu*, *hoisin*, *ko*, *kuei*, *kwai-lo*, *lei*, *ling chih*, *mee*, *mei ping*, *pai-hua*, *pakapoo*, *p'an*, *putonghua*, *qinghaosu*, *samfu*, *san ts'ai*, *subgum*, *tu-mo*, *ve-tsin*, *wen jen*, *wen-yen*, *wushu*, *wu ts'ai*, *ying ch'ing*, *yuan*.

## 4.3 Chinese Loanwords in General English Dictionaries

The words of foreign origins become institutionalized and accepted into the vocabulary of a language when they are recorded in general dictionaries. When it comes to the selection of entries, the criteria for currency usually suggests a bias in favor of words that are still widely used. For the consideration of general use, the words should be encountered in non-specialist literature.

*The Oxford English Dictionary* (OED), published by the Oxford University Press, is one of the largest and most comprehensive dictionary of the English language. It covers words from across the English-speaking world, and traces the development of English from the earliest records to the present day. It is an unsurpassed guide to the meaning, history, and pronunciation of 600,000 words. Some of these words are now obsolete, but most are not. Although a total count of over 600,000 (including simplex, compounds and derivative formations) lexemes is vast, the OED should not be taken as a catalogue of every word or expression that ever is or has been used in English. The OED's selection criteria for including lexemes pay careful attention to questions of frequency of use and spread in different contexts of use, and its wordlist can be taken as a good reflection of those words that have had most impact on the lexicon of English since the mid-12th century. The OED has been compiled over a very long time: the first edition was published in fascicles (or instalments) between 1884 and 1928; supplements were added in 1933 and (in four volumes) between 1972 and 1986; and these were brought together with the main text in the Second Edition of 1989. At present the dictionary is undergoing its first thoroughgoing revision and update. 70 editors are updating the text of the dictionary for its Third Edition. OED Online was launched as a digital companion to OED. It offers access to OED in its most recent version and is updated every three months to provide users with the results of the current research and revision of the editors.

Durkin (2014) lists the most frequent donor languages to English. Chinese is among the most frequent 25 donor languages (see Figures 4.1 and 4.2).

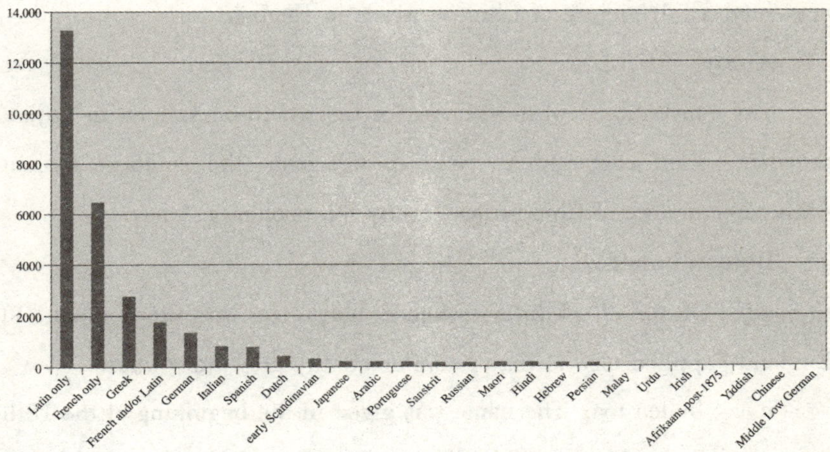


Figure 4.1 Totals of loanwords from the 25 most prolific inputs in OED3 (Durkin, 2014: 25)

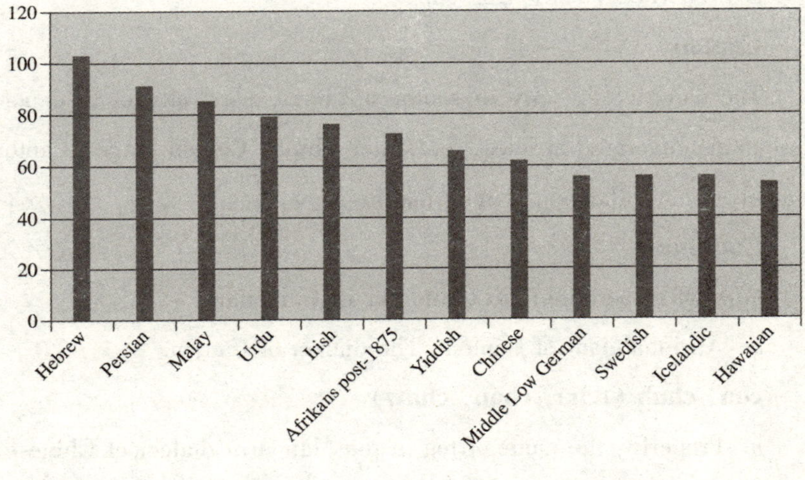


Figure 4.2 The position of Chinese in the most frequent donor languages (Durkin, 2014: 27)

Here we surveyed the OED (the CD-ROM version), and picked out the words which are indicated as Chinese origin. These words have presented a full picture of Chinese words in English.

**Amoy**

The conventional western name for the island of Xiamen in Fujian province, south-east China, used to designate the southern Fujian (Minnan) dialect of Chinese spoken by the people of Amoy.

**Bohea(bohee)**

*adj.* Of the Wu-i hills, whence black tea was first brought to England; applied also to tea of similar quality grown elsewhere.

*n.* = Bohea tea. The name was given in the beginning of the 18th c. to the finest kinds of black tea; but the quality now known as "Bohea" is the lowest, being the last crop of the season.

**campoi**

A fired variety of Congou tea.

**Canton**

The name of the city in southern China, used attrib. to denote various manufactured articles, as Canton china, Canton crape, Canton enamel, Canton flannel, Canton matting.

**Cantonese**

*adj.* Of or pertaining to Canton or its inhabitants.

*n.* An inhabitant of Canton; The dialect of Canton.

**cha, chah (tcha, chau, chaw)**

*n.* Properly, the name of tea in the Mandarin dialect of Chinese, which was occasionally used in English at the first introduction of the beverage. (Some subsequently applied it as a name to the special form of rolled tea used in Central Asia.) Now used slang for tea.

**chen shu**

*n.* Also Chêng-Shu, Chincù Chinese zhēnshū, a type of writing.

**cheongsam (cheong sam, chong-sam)**

A garment worn by Chinese women.

**Ch'ien Lung**

The name of the Emperor of China who reigned 1736-1796, used to designate pottery, carved jade, etc., made during those years, or the period itself.

**chin chin (chin-chin)**

A phrase of salutation. Also used as a drinking toast; to salute, greet.

**chop-chop**

An imitation of a natural sound.

**chop-suey**

A Chinese dish of meat or chicken, rice, onions, etc., fried in sesame-oil.

**chow mein**

Fried noodles served with a thick sauce or stew composed of chopped meat, vegetables, etc.

**Confucian**

*adj.* of or relating to the Chinese philosopher Confucius, or his teaching, or followers.

*n.* A follower of Confucius.

**Confucianism**

The doctrine or system of Confucius and his followers.

**dim sum (deem sim, tim-sam, tim-sum)**

A savoury Cantonese-style snack; a meal consisting of these dotchin (dodgeon, dodging).

**erh hu** ( **ellhwu**, **erh-hu**, **erhu** )

A Chinese two-stringed fiddle.

**fan-tan**

A Chinese gambling game, in which a number of small coins are placed under a bowl and the players then bet as to what will be the remainder when the pile has been divided by four.

**fen** ( **fan**, **fun** )

A Chinese monetary unit equivalent to one hundredth of a yuan or one tenth of a jiao; formerly, a candareen. Also, a coin of this value.

**feng-shui** ( **fong-choui** )

In Chinese mythology, a system of spirit influences, good and evil, which inhabit the natural features of landscapes; hence, a kind of geomancy for dealing with these influences in determining sites for houses and graves.

**fum** ( **fung** )

A fabulous bird ( by Europeans commonly called the phoenix ), one of the symbols of the imperial dignity in China.

**fu yung** ( **fooyong**, **foo yong**, **yoong**, **fu-yung** )

A Chinese sauce made with eggs mixed and cooked with a variety of other ingredients. Usu. in the name of the dish with which the sauce is served, as egg fu yung, etc.

**Hakka**

A member of a people now dwelling in parts of southern China, especially in the province of Kwangtung or Canton, and in Taiwan, Hong Kong, etc. Also the dialect spoken by this people.

**Han**

Designating a Chinese dynasty ( 206 b. c. - 220 a. d. ) marked by the introduction of Buddhism, the extension of Chinese rule over Mongolia, the revival of letters, and increase of wealth and culture.

**hao**

[Vietnamese hào, (Chinese háo) one hundredth of a (Chinese) ounce.] In Vietnam, a monetary unit equal to one-tenth of a dong, introduced in 1885 and formally discontinued by 1986; a coin or note of this value.

**hien, hsien (heen)**

An administrative division of a fu or department, or of an independent chow or district. Also, the seat of government of such a division.

**hoey**

A society of Chinese: esp. a secret society formed by them in English-speaking countries or colonies.

**Hoisin**

Fresh seafood, seafood in general. More fully hoisin sauce. A rich, sweet, dark sauce made from soya beans, garlic, vegetable extracts, and spices, widely used in Chinese cookery.

**Hokkien**

Of, relating to, or designating a dialect of Southern Min traditionally spoken in south-eastern China, and now one of the major Chinese dialects of Malaysia, Singapore, Taiwan, and the Philippines. The northern and southern varieties of Hokkien together with Amoy form the subdialect Xiamen.

Of, relating to, or designating a member of a Chinese people traditionally inhabiting south-eastern China who speak a dialect of Southern Min, or their culture or cuisine.

The Hokkien dialect of Southern Min. A member of the Hokkien people.

**Honan**

The name of a province of Northern China, used to designate: (a) a variety of silk manufactured there; (b) ceramics of the Song dynasty, probably manufactured there.

**hong** (**haung**)

In China, a series of rooms or buildings used as a warehouse, factory, etc.; spec. (a) one of the foreign factories formerly maintained at Canton; (b) the corporation of Chinese merchants at Canton who (before the treaty of Nanking in 1842) had the monopoly of trade with Europeans; (c) a foreign trading establishment in China or Japan.

**hoppo**

In China: The board of revenue or customs. Also (short for hoppo-man) an officer of the customs.

**Hunanese**

Of, pertaining to, or characteristic of Hunan or of the Chinese spoken there.

An inhabitant of Hunan. The dialect of Hunan.

**Hutung**

In northern Chinese cities: a narrow side-street, an alley.

**hyson**

A species of green tea from China. Young hyson, a fine green tea.

**I Ching**

[Book of Changes] The name of an ancient Chinese divination manual, based on symbols known as the eight trigrams and sixty-four hexagrams.

**jiao (chiao)**

A unit of currency and coin of China.

**jiaozi**

In Chinese cookery: a crescent-shaped dumpling of thin pastry dough, stuffed with a finely minced paste (typically made of pork, cabbage, and garlic chives), and steam-fried, deep-fried, grilled, or boiled.

**jong (dzong)**

A Tibetan building (also, a territorial and administrative division) constituting a prefecture, freq. also serving as a fortress, a monastery, or both. Hence dzongpön, jongpen, jong-pon, a prefect; jong-nyer, a sub-prefect.

**K'ai shu**

The standard calligraphic script used for the Chinese language, developed during the Later Han dynasty (23-220) as a simplified form of the official li-shu script.

**K'ang-Hsi**

[Royal name of Hsüan-Yeh, emperor of China 1661-1722.] Used. with reference to the Chinese pottery and porcelain of the latter half of the seventeenth century and the first quarter of the eighteenth, notable for very fine blue-and-white wares and the development of famille verte and famille noire enamels.

**kaoliang**

[Chinese; lit. "high grain".] The Indian millet, Sorghum vulgare.

**kaolin**

A fine white clay produced by the decomposition of feldspar, used in the manufacture of porcelain; first employed by the Chinese, but subsequently obtained also in Cornwall, Saxony, France (near Limoges), United States, etc.

**ketchup (kitchup, catchup)**

(Chinese Amoy dialect, kôechiap or kê-tsiap) Malay kēchap, which has been claimed as the original source (Scott Malayan Wds. in English 64-67), may be from Chinese. A sauce made from the juice of mushrooms, walnuts, tomatoes, etc., and used as a condiment with meat, fish, or the like. Often with qualification, as mushroom ketchup, etc.

**Khamba**

Tibetan people from Kham; one of this people.

The language spoken by this people.

**khatak (khata, khatag)**

In Tibet, a scarf presented to visitors.

**Khotan (Khoten)**

Name of a city and district on the south of the Takla Makan desert in Chinese Turkestan, used attrib. and ellipt. to designate a carpet or rug made there, usu. with Chinese geometrical patterns or stylized natural designs.

**kiang (kyang)**

A species or sub-species of equine quadruped (Equus kiang), a wild horse or ass, inhabiting the high table-lands of Tibet.

**Kiangsi (Kiang-si)**

*n.* [Chinese Jiāngxī the name of a province in S. E. China] attrib. Designating or pertaining to the period of communist rule in this province from 1929 to 1934, esp. the independent soviet republic established by Mao Zedong in 1931.

**Kiasu**

*n.* and *a.* colloq. (chiefly in South-East Asia, esp. Singapore). Depreciative. [Chinese (Hokkien) kiasu, lit. "scared to lose"]

*n.* A person governed by self-interest, typically manifesting as a selfish, grasping attitude arising from a fear of missing out on something. Also such an attitude.

*adj.* Chiefly of a person: characterized by a grasping or selfish attitude arising from a fear of missing out on something.

**kittisol**

A sunshade, parasol, umbrella: almost always in reference to the East Indies or China; spec. a Chinese umbrella made of bamboo and oiled paper.

**Ko Ceramics**

Ko ware. A crackled Song ware closely related to Southern Kuan; also, a name for other crackled porcelains.

**Ko (ge)**

[Chinese gē (Wade-Giles ko) spear, lance.] A weapon that can be used as both a dagger and an axe; a halberd.

**kongsi**

[kung-ssu (as pronounced in Hokkien) company, corporation.] In Malaysia, an association or partnership, esp. an association of Chinese people.

**kow-tow (kotow, kow-too, ko-too, ko-tou, ka-tou, koo-too)**

*n.* The Chinese custom of touching the ground with the forehead in the act of prostrating oneself, as an expression of extreme respect, submission, or worship.

**kraak porcelein** (**kraakporselein kraak porcelain**)

Blue-and-white Chinese porcelain of the Wan-li period (1573-1619) or later in the seventeenth century, or a European imitation of this.

**Kuan** (**Kwan**)

[Chinese guān, kuān official.] Used to denote imperial patronage or official usage in China, as:

Kuan Hua[language, speech] = mandarin.

Kuan Yin [Lord of Mercy], a goddess of Chinese Buddhism, to whom intercession for aid or protection is made; a representation in sculpture of this deity.

Kuan ware, Kuanyao [jade]. A type of thickly glazed celadon made in predominantly greyish colours at Hangchow during the Sung dynasty; similar pottery (as the Kuan jar) produced elsewhere in China in later centuries.

**kuei**

A Chinese bronze food-vessel.

**kumquat** (**cumquat, camquit**)

[The Cantonese dialectal form of the Chinese name kin kü "gold orange"] A small, orange-like citrus fruit from a tree of the genus Fortunella, native to southern China and Malaysia.

**Kung-fu** (**kung-fu, kungfu**)

[Chinese] The Chinese form of karate. Also attrib.

**Kuomintang**

[lit. "national people's party".] A nationalist radical party founded in China under Sun Yat-Sen in 1912, and led, after his death in 1925, by Chiang Kai-Shek, constituting the government before the Communist Party took power in October 1949, and subsequently forming the central administration of Taiwan.

**Kuo-yü (kuojy, Guoryu, Kuoyu)**

The name given to the Chinese "national tongue", a form of Mandarin adopted for official use.

**kwai-lo(kwailo, kwai-tze)**

"Foreign devil", a name given by the Chinese to foreigners.

**kylin(kilin)**

[Chinese ch'i-lin (Wade), ch'i male + lin female.] A fabulous animal of composite form, commonly figured on Chinese and Japanese pottery.

**Lah**

int. [Chinese (southern dial.).] In Singaporean English, a particle used with various kinds of pitch to convey the mood and attitude of the speaker.

**Lahu (La Hu, La-hu)**

(A member of) a minority people of the Lolo group in S. W. China, esp. Yunnan.

The Tibeto-Burman language of this people.

**Langshan**

[Name of a locality about fifty miles from Shanghai; in Chinese = "wolf hill".] A breed of domestic fowl, introduced from China.

**lei**

[Chinese léi.] An urn-shaped Chinese bronze wine-vessel of the Shang to Middle Chou period.

**lei wên(lei-wan, leiwen)**

*n.* Ceramics. [Chinese léi wén, lit. "thunder symbol". ] A spiral fret motif often used to form a background or decorative filler on ancient Chinese bronze or ceramic wares.

**li (lii, le)**

The ordinary Chinese itinerary measure.

**li**

An ancient Chinese cooking vessel of bronze or pottery with usu. three hollow legs.

**liang (leang)**

A Chinese weight, about 11/3 oz. avoirdupois; this weight in silver as a money of account. Also called tael.

**likin (lekin)**

A Chinese provincial transit duty.

**ling**

The water-chestnut of China, Trapa bicornis, the seeds of which are much eaten as food.

**ling chih (lingzhi)**

The fungus Ganoderma lucidum, believed in China to confer longevity and used as a symbol of this on Chinese ceramic ware.

**li shu**

An ancient Chinese calligraphic script developed during the Han dynasty (206 b. c.-200 a. d.) and widely adopted for official and educational purposes.

**Lisu**

*n.* A member of a people indigenous to the mountainous south-western region of China; an ethnic sub-group of the Yi; The Tibeto-

Burman language of this people.

*adj.* Of, pertaining to, or concerned with the Lisu or their language.

**litchi** (**leeche**, **leechee**, **li-chee**, **lichi**, **li-chi**, **lychee**)

The fruit of an evergreen tree, Litchi chinensis, of the family Sapindaceae, native to southern China but widely cultivated in tropical countries elsewhere; the fruit is a large berry with a rough, brown skin and sweet, white flesh, which is eaten fresh or preserved.

**li ting** (**liding**, **li-ting**)

An ancient (usu. tripodal) Chinese bronze or pottery cooking vessel with solid legs.

**Lohan = Arhat**, **Arahat**

A Buddhist saint of the highest rank.

**Lolo**

The name of an aboriginal people of south-western China, of a member of this people, and of their Tibeto-Burmese language.

**longan** (**lungung**, **lungan**, **lung-yen**)

The fruit of an evergreen tree, Nephelium Longanum, cultivated in China and the East Indies. Also, the tree itself.

**loquat** (**lacott**, **loquet**, **loquette**, **loquot**)

The fruit of Eriobotrya japonica, a native of China and Japan, introduced into southern Europe, India, and Australia.

The tree itself. Also loquat tree.

**lü** (**liu**, **liuh**)

In ancient Chinese musical theory, a fundamental pitch; any of the twelve pitches in an untempered chromatic scale; also used attrib. to refer to (each of) a series of bamboo pipes used to produce these pitches. In Chinese, although known collectively as the twelve lǜ, there are two separate characters; lǜ for the odd-numbered pitches, and lǚ for the even-numbered.

**Lung-ch'üan**

The name of a district in the province of Chekiang, China, used to designate a type of Chinese celadon ware produced mainly during the Song dynasty (960-1279).

**Lung-shan** (**Longshan**, **Lung Shan**, **Lungshan**)

Archaeol. [The name of a town in the Shandong province of eastern China.] Used to designate a Neolithic Chinese culture of 3000-2500 b. c. , and its artefacts (spec. a fine, burnished black pottery), evidence of which was first unearthed at Lung-shan in 1928.

**ly** (**variant of li**)

Chinese land-measure.

**Macanese** (**Macaoese Macaonese**)

*n.* A native or inhabitant of Macao, a city and Portuguese dependency on the south-east coast of China, esp. one of mixed Chinese and Portuguese descent.

The Portuguese-based creole language spoken in Macao.

*adj.* Of or pertaining to Macao or the Macanese.

**mafoo** (**ma-fu**)

A Chinese groom, stable-boy, or coachman.

**Manchu** (**Manchew**, **Manchoo**, **Manchow**, **Mantcheou**, **Mantchoo**, **Mantchu**)

*n.* A member of a Tungusic race inhabiting Manchuria, which conquered China in 1644 and was the ruling class until the Revolution in 1912.

The language of the Manchus.

*adj.* Of or pertaining to the Manchus, their country (Manchuria), or their language.

**Mandarin** (**mandeline**, **mandorijn**, **mandarim**, **mandorin**, **mandarine**, **mandareen**)

*n.* A generic name for all grades of Chinese officials; there were nine ranks, each of which was distinguished by a particular kind of "button".

A toy representing a grotesque seated figure in Chinese costume, so contrived as to continue nodding for a long time after it is shaken.

A person of much importance, a great man. Often used colloq. of government officials, leading politicians or writers, etc.

(With capital initial.) The language spoken in China by officials and educated people generally. Hence, any of the varieties of Kuan Hua or Mandarin spoken as a common language in China, spec. the Northern variety, which forms the basis of putonghua; = putonghua.

Short for mandarin porcelain.

*adj.* attrib., as (1) mandarin boat, mandarin dignity, mandarin governor, mandarin promotion, mandarin sepulchre; (2) mandarin Chinese, mandarin dialect, mandarin glossary, mandarin language, mandarin tongue; mandarin blue; mandarin broth; mandarin cap, a child's cap resembling that worn by a mandarin; mandarin cat, a kind of Angora cat; mandarin coat; mandarin collar, a narrow collar standing up from a close-fitting neckline; mandarin duck, a duck of bright and variegated plumage, Aix galericulate, native to China; mandarin hat, one shaped like that worn by mandarins; mandarin jar, a jar of mandarin porcelain; mandarin porcelain, Japanese porcelain decorated with figures of mandarins; mandarin sleeve, a wide loose sleeve copied from the sleeves of the dress of mandarins; mandarin vase, a vase of mandarin porcelain.

**Mao**

[Mao Tse-Tung] Used attrib. of a simple style of clothing based on dress in Communist China, as Mao cap, Mao collar, Mao jacket, Mao trousers, etc.

**Maoism**

[the name of Mao Tse-Tung (1893-1976), Chairman of the Central Committee of the Chinese Communist Party + -ism.] The Marxist-Leninist theories of Mao Tse-Tung developed and practised in China.

**Mao tai (Mao Tai, mao-tai, Mao-T'ai, Maotai)**

[Maotai, name of a town in south-west China.] A mellow and strong pot-stilled spirit produced in Maotai.

**Miao (Meo)**

*n.* A member of the Miao, a mountain-dwelling people of China and Indo-China; the Miao people; the language spoken by the Miao.

*adj.* Of or pertaining to the Miao people or their language.

**Ming**

The name of a dynasty which ruled in China from 1368 to 1644; a ruler belonging to this dynasty. Also attrib.

Used attrib. and absol. of the porcelain of the Ming period (of which the finest examples are extremely rare and valuable).

Used attrib. to denote colours characteristic of Ming porcelain, as Ming blue, Ming green, Ming yellow.

**mou** ( **mow**, **mu** )

A Chinese unit of area, varying according to locality but usually equivalent to about 670 square metres (800 square yards).

**Moutan**

The tree peony, Paeonia suffruticosa, of the family Ranunculaceae, a large shrub bearing pale pink flowers, native to China, the parent of many garden varieties producing single or double flowers of many colours.

**pai-hua** ( **bai hua**, **báihuà** )

The standard written form of modern Chinese, based on the northern dialects, esp. that of Peking; the vernacular literary style (opp. wenyen). Also attrib.

**Pailou**

An elaborate Chinese commemorative or ornamental gateway.

**pakapoo** ( **pakapu**, **pak-a-peu**, **puka pu** )

Chinese gambling game resembling lottery with sheets of paper so marked as to be indecipherable except to an initiate.

**pak-choi**

A Chinese species of cabbage, Brassica chinensis. Also attrib.

**paktong** ( **packtong** )

Chinese nickel-silver; an alloy of copper, zinc, and nickel, resembling silver.

**pa-kua** ( **ba gua**, **pa kua**, **pa-kwa** )

Any of various traditional Chinese symbols or motifs incorporating the eight trigrams of the I Ching; spec. an arrangement of these trigrams in a circle round the yin-yang symbol.

A Chinese system of unarmed combat and physical training,

involving boxing, and characterized by continuous walking in a circle.

**pao-chia** (**pao chia**, **paochia**)

In China, a system by which households were organized for the purposes of administration. Also attrib.

**pao-tzu** (**bao zi**)

A steamed roll with savoury or sweet fillings.

**Peking, Pekin**

The name of the capital of China; hence, applied attrib. or elliptically.

A kind of silk stuff.

A type of Chinese rug or carpet.

Attrib. & Comb., as Peking carpet, Peking crepe, Peking rug; Peking duck, (a) a large white duck with yellow bill and legs, belonging to a breed imported from China to Britain and the U. S. A. in 1873; (b) a speciality of Chinese cuisine; Peking Labrador; Peking man, a fossil hominid, Homo erectus pekinensis, first described in 1926 from remains found in caves near the village of Choukoutien; Peking opera, a stylized form of opera which evolved in China during the nineteenth century; Peking point; Peking spaniel = Pekin(g)ese.

**Pekin(g)ese**

A native or inhabitant of Peking.

The form of Chinese used in Peking.

A Pekingese dog.

*adj.* Of or pertaining to Peking; applied esp. to a breed of dwarf pug-dogs with long, silky hair, obtained originally from the Imperial Palace at Peking; Pekingese stitch, a stitch in embroidery.

**pe-tsai**

A Chinese species of cabbage, Brassica pekinensis. Also attrib.

**Pinyin (Pin-yin, Pin-Yin)**

A system of Romanized spelling for the Chinese language, adopted officially by the People's Republic of China in stages since 1958. Also attrib.

**p'ip'a (pepa, pipa)**

A Chinese stringed instrument.

**po shan lu (bo shan lu)**

A type of Chinese bronze censer, made during the Han dynasty and having the form of a mythical mountain of immortality.

**potsticker**

A filled dumpling, typically crescent-shaped, esp. one that is pan-fried until brown on one side, then turned and simmered in a small amount of broth.

**putonghua (p'ut'ung-hua)**

The standard spoken language now in general use throughout the People's Republic of China, based on the northern dialects, esp. that of Peking.

**qi (ch'i, Qi)**

The physical life-force postulated by certain Chinese philosophers; the material principle.

**Qinghaosu**

A naturally-occurring sesquiterpenoid compound, extracted from the Chinese plant Artemisia annua, which has been used to treat malaria; = artemisinin.

**Red Army**

The name given to the Russian Bolshevik army and later to that of the Soviet Union. Adopted as the name of the army in other, esp. communist countries.

**Red China**

Communist China; the People's Republic of China. Hence Red Chinese.

**renminbi (jenminpi, renminpi, Renminbi)**

The name of the currency introduced in China in 1948.

Occas. used for yuan, the basic unit of this currency.

**rolwagen (rollwagon, rolwaggon, row-waggon)**

A kind of Chinese cylindrical porcelain vase, or a Dutch imitation of this.

**samfu (samfoo)**

[Cantonese] A suit consisting of jacket and trousers worn by Chinese women, particularly in Malaysia and Hong Kong; also worn by men. Freq. attrib., as samfu jacket, samfu trousers.

**sampan (champana, champan, sampane, siampan, sampaan, sampang, sanpan)**

A Chinese word meaning "boat", applied by Europeans in the China seas to any small boat of Chinese pattern.

**samshoo (sam shu, samptsoo, samshew, samshue, samso, samsu, samtchoo)**

The general name for Chinese spirits distilled from rice or sorghum.

**Sanfan (San-fan, San Fan)**

Used attrib. to designate an official campaign conducted in China in 1951-1952 against corruption, waste, and bureaucratism in State affairs.

**sang-de-boeuf**

A deep red colour found on old Chinese porcelain. A ceramic glaze of this colour; porcelain bearing such a glaze. Also attrib.

**san hsien** (**san heen**, **san hien**, **san-hsien**)

A Chinese three-stringed plucked instrument with a long neck and oval-shaped body.

**san ts'ai**

Chinese pottery, esp. of the Tang dynasty, decorated in three colours; decoration in three enamel colours applied to pottery and porcelain. Also attrib.

**se** (**che**, **she**, **tche**)

A twenty-five-stringed plucked musical instrument, somewhat similar to the zither. This ancient instrument was already widely used during the Spring and Warring States period (770-476 b. c.). The number of strings was not fixed in ancient times.

**senshaw**

A Chinese gauze-like silk fabric.

**Shang** (**Chang**, **Xanga**)

The name of a dynasty which ruled China during part of the second millennium b. c., probably from the 16th to the 11th century b. c. Also attrib. or as adj. Also called Shang-Yin [the place-name Yin in Henan Province, the dynasty's final capital].

**Shanghainese**

[Shanghai (see shanghai *n.*) + -n- + -ese, after Chinese, etc.] The Chinese dialect of the Wu group spoken in Shanghai; a native or inhabitant of Shanghai (also collect.).

**Shantung**

[The name of a province of North-east China where it is manufactured.] A soft undressed silk (formerly undyed, since 1907 dyed to any shade of colour).

**Shaolin**

[Shàolínsì, the name of a Buddhist monastery in the Henan Province of China, built in the late 5th cent. a. d.] Any of various styles or schools of Chinese martial arts developed by or popularly associated with the monks of the Shaolin monastery.

**Shar-Pei** (**Shar Pei**, **Sharpe**)

A breed of compact, squarely built dogs of Chinese origin, with a characteristic loose, deeply wrinkled skin and a short, bristly coat of a cream, fawn, red, or black colour; a dog of this breed.

**shen** (**Shen**, **Shin**)

In Chinese philosophy: a god, person of supernatural power, or the spirit of a dead person.

**sheng** (**cheng**, **sang**, **sing**)

A Chinese wind instrument consisting of a set of reed pipes.

**Sinetic** (**Sinitic**)

*adj.* Chinese. [late L. Sin-ae (see Sinaean) + -itic.]

**Sinic** (**Sinick**)

*adj.* Chinese.

**sinseh**

[ad. Malay sinse, variant of singse, sengse, sengsai Chinese physician, prob. ad. Chinese dial. (Changchew) sin-sen (Chinese xiānsheng), Amoy sien-sin teacher, mister, sir, doctor.] In

Malaysia, Singapore, and Indonesia: a traditional Chinese physician or herbalist.

**souchong**

(Cantonese siu chung) small sort. One of the finer varieties of black tea. Also attrib.

**suan-pan (souan-, shwan-, swam-, swan-)**

[Reckoning board.] The Chinese abacus.

**Sui (Suy, Swi)**

The name of a dynasty which ruled in China from 581 to 618 and re-unified the country after the divisions of the Northern and Southern Dynasties period.

**Sung (Sunga, Song)**

The name of a dynasty which ruled in China from 960 to 1279; a member of this dynasty. Also attrib. of the arts, design, and porcelain of the Sung period.

**Sun Yat-sen (Sun Yatsen)**

The Cantonese form of the personal name Sun I-xian, adopted by Sun Wen (1866-1925), founder in 1911 of the Republic of China, used attrib. to designate a modern style of clothing in China.

**sycee (sisee, seze)**

Fine uncoined silver in the form of lumps of various sizes, usually having a banker's or assayer's seal stamped on them, formerly used by the Chinese as a medium of exchange. Also sycee silver.

**Szechuan (Szechwan)**

The name of a province in south-western China, used attrib. (with reversed stress) to designate the distinctively spicy cuisine originating there. Also Comb., as Szechuan-style adj. Also transf.

**Sze Yap（Sze-Yap, Szeyap）**

The name of an area made up of four countries in the south of Guangdong Province in China. used attrib. and absol. to designate the Chinese dialect spoken there.

**ta chuan（ta tchuen）**

In Chinese calligraphy, an early form of script used during the Zhou Dynasty; "large seal script".

**tael（taile, tayel, tayl, tale, tahel, tahil, tay, taye）**

[The early tay, taes, etc. represent the Pg. plural.] The trade name for the Chinese liang or "ounce", a weight used in China and the East. In Chinese use the liang varies according to local custom, and to the commodity weighed; but the weight of 11/3 oz. avoirdupois is fixed by treaty for commercial purposes.

Hence, A money of account, originally a tael (in weight) of standard silver, the value of which fluctuates with the price of the metal.

**T'ai Chi（Tai Chi, t'ai chi）**

In Taoism and Neo-Confucianism, the Supreme Ultimate. Also, the symbol which represents this.

In full T'ai Chi Ch'uan [Chinese quan fist], a Chinese martial art, believed to have been devised by a Taoist priest in the Sung dynasty (960-1279), promoting meditative as well as physical proficiency.

**taikonaut（Draft entry February 2007）**

[Apparently a blend of Chinese *tai kong* outer space and astronaut. Compare cosmonaut] A Chinese astronaut.

**taipan** ( **taepan**, **typan** )

A foreign merchant or businessman in China. The ( foreign ) manager or head of a firm in China, esp. Hong Kong.

**Tai-ping** ( **Taë-ping** )

The name given to the adherents of a great rebellion which arose in Southern China in 1850, under the leadership of Hung-siu-tsuen, styled Tien-wang, Heavenly Prince, and T'ai-p'ing-wang, Prince of great peace, who claimed a divine commission to overthrow the Manchu dynasty and establish one of native origin, to be called the T'ai-p'ing Chao or Great Peace Dynasty. Also attrib. Hence Tai-pingdom, Tai-pingism. The war which ensued devastated some of the most fertile provinces of China for a number of years; partly by means of English help the Tai-pings were finally routed and dispersed in 1865.

**tan** ( **dan** )

A female character in a Chinese drama or opera; an actor of such a role.

**Tang** ( **T'ang**, **Tanga** )

The name of a dynasty which ruled in China from 618 to 906; a ruler belonging to this dynasty.

Attrib. or as *adj.* Freq. used to designate artefacts, etc. , of this period.

**tangpu** ( **Tang Pu** )

The headquarters of the Kuomintang at the central, and various local, levels.

**Tanka** ( **tankia**, **tanchia** )

The boat-population of Canton, who live entirely on the boats by which they earn their living: they are descendants of some aboriginal tribe of which Tan was apparently the name. Tanka boat, a boat of the kind in which these people live.

**tao (Dao, Tao, taou, tau)**

[Chinese dào (Wade-Giles tao) way, path, right way (of life), reason.] In Taoism, an absolute entity which is the source of the universe; the way in which this absolute entity functions.

= Taoism, Taoist

In Confucianism and in extended uses, the way to be followed, the right conduct; doctrine or method.

**Taoism (Daoism)**

A system of religion, founded upon the doctrine of the ancient Chinese philosopher Laotsze (or Lao-tz'), born 604 b. c., set forth in the work *Tao tê king*, "Book of reason and virtue", attributed to him. It ranks with Confucianism and Buddhism as one of the three religions of China.

**Taoist (Daoist)**

An adherent of Taoism. Of or belonging to the Taoists or to Taoism.

**Tao Kuang (Daoguang)**

The title of the reign of Xuan Zong (Min-Ning), emperor of China 1821-1850, used to designate the period of his reign or pottery and porcelain made at this time.

**taotai (Taotai, tautai)**

The title given to the Chinese provincial officer responsible for the civil and military affairs of a district, abolished shortly after the establishment of the Republic in 1911.

**t'ao t'ieh** ( **taotie**, **tao-tieh** )

The name of a mythical monster, or a mask-design showing its face, found esp. on metalware of the Chou period (1122-221 b. c. ).

**te** ( **Te**, **teh**, **tih** )

In Taoism, the essence of Tao inherent in all beings.

In Confucianism and in extended use, moral virtue.

**tiao** ( **tiaou** )

A string of Chinese "cash" (perforated copper coins). Nominally the tiao contained 1,000 cash; but the actual number of coins varied from 1,000 downwards, according to the custom of the locality.

**t'ien** ( **tayn**, **tyen**, **tien** )

In Chinese thought: Heaven; the Deity.

**ting**

An ancient Chinese vessel, usu. bronze, having two looped handles and three or four legs.

**ti-tzu** ( **Ti tzu** )

A type of Chinese bamboo flute.

**tofu**

A curd made in Japan and China from mashed soya beans; bean curd.

**tou** ( **dou** )

A hemispherical pedestaled bowl with a lid of similar shape, used as a container for food.

**tou ts'ai** ( **tu tsai**, **doucai** )

Used attrib. and absol. of a kind of enamel painting on Chinese porcelain, developed in the reign of Ch'êng Hua (1465-1487), and of (pieces of) porcelain so decorated.

**ts'ao shu（cao shu, tsaou shoo）**

In Chinese calligraphy, a cursive script developed during the Han dynasty（206 b. c. -220 a. d.）from the "official" script.

**Tsu**

A patrilineal kinship group in pre-revolutionary China. According to accepted principle, all the patrilineal descendants and their wives that can be traced to a common ancestor within five kinship grades consider themselves as belonging to a kinship group called Tsu.

**Tsun**

A style of Chinese vessel, either wide-mouthed or animal-shaped.

**tsung（ts'ung）**

A ritual artefact（usu. made of a single piece of jade）consisting of a hollow cylinder with a central rectangular section, found esp. in graves of the Shang-Zhou period（16th-11th cent. b. c.）, and regarded as a symbol of, or sacrificial offering to, the Earth.

**tuchun（Tuchun, Tu Chün）**

In China at the time of the Three Kingdoms, the title of a military leader; later, in the early years of the Republic of China, the highest military leader in a province; a warlord.

**tui na（tuina; Draft entry June 2007）**

In traditional Chinese medicine: a type of therapeutic massage, incorporating the principles of acupressure and qigong, used to treat muscle or joint pain and other ailments.

**tu-mo（Tu Mu）**

In Chinese medical theory, the chief passage through which the vital energy circulates, located within the spine; spec. in acupuncture.

**tung (tung-yu, tung oil)**

Any of three trees of the genus Aleurites or Vernicia (family Euphorbiaceae), which are native to China and Japan and are cultivated there and elsewhere for the oil from their seeds.

The oil extracted from seeds of the tung tree, used chiefly in the manufacture of inks, paints, and varnishes; = wood-oil (c). attrib., as tung nut; tung oil, a drying oil obtained from the seeds of tung trees and used in varnishes, paints, and inks; so tung oil tree.

**tupan**

The civil governor of a Chinese province under the Republican regime.

**typhoon**

A violent cyclonic storm or hurricane occuring in the China seas and adjacent regions, chiefly during the period from July to October.

**Tz'u Chou**

Pottery made at Tz'u Chou (Cizhou), or in similar styles elsewhere, from the Sui dynasty onwards.

**ve-tsin (veh t'sin)**

Monosodium glutamate, a flavour enhancer frequently used in Chinese cookery.

**wei ch'i (wei chi)**

A traditional Chinese board game of territorial possession, equivalent to *go*.

**wên jên**

Chinese men of letters.

**wen li = wen-yen**

The synonymy is based on a misconception of the Chinese

meaning, and does not exist in that language.

**wen-yen** (**wenyan, wenyen**)

The traditional literary language or style of China, superseded in the twentieth century by pai-hua.

**Wing Chun**

A simplified form of kung-fu used principally as a system of self-defence.

**wok** (**wock**)

A bowl-shaped pan used in Chinese cookery.

**won ton** (**wan tan, wun tun, and as one word**)

A small round roll or pocket of dough containing a savoury filling, eaten alone (after being deep-fried) or boiled in soup (won ton soup).

**wushu** (**wu shu and with capital initial**)

The Chinese martial arts.

**wu-wei** (**Woo-wei, wu wei**)

The Taoist doctrine of letting things follow their own course.

In China, the name of a minor sect.

**yamun**(**yamen**)

The office or official residence of a Chinese mandarin; hence, any department of the Chinese public service, as the tsung li yamun or Chinese "foreign office", established in 1860.

**yang ch'in** (**yang ching, jin, kin, and as one word**)

A Chinese musical instrument similar to the dulcimer.

**yang-ko** (**yangko and as two words**)

A type of folk-dance popular in northern China.

**Yang-shao** (**Yang Shao, Yang shao**)

The name of a village in the Henan province of China, used to designate a Neolithic Chinese culture (5000-3000 b. c.), and its artefacts, evidence of which was first discovered there in 1921.

**Yarkand**

[The name of a river, district, and city in Sinkiang Uighur (formerly Chinese Turkestan), an autonomous region of western China.] A language or dialect of the central Turkic or Turco-Tatar group of Altaic languages, spoken in the district of Yarkand. Used to designate a type of Turkoman carpet.

Also used to designate a heavily built kind of red deer with short antlers that is found in Sinkiang Uighur.

**yen(yin, ying)**

(U. S. slang) The most likely etymon is Chinese (Cantonese) yǎn craving; the forms yin and ying may reflect the Mandarin pronunciation yǐn of the same character.

The craving of a drug-addict for his drug (orig. for opium).

A craving, a yearning or longing.

*v.* intr., to crave for a drug; to yearn, desire strongly;

yenny *a.*, affected by a craving for drugs.

**yen-yen**

(U. S. slang) A craving for opium, the "opium-habit".

**yin (Yin, Yn)**

In Chinese philosophy, the feminine or negative principle (characterized by dark, wetness, cold, passivity, disintegration, etc.) of the two opposing cosmic forces into which creative energy divides and whose fusion in physical matter brings the phenomenal world into being.

Comb., as yin-yang, the combination or fusion of the two cosmic forces; freq. attrib., esp. as yin-yang symbol, a circle divided by an

S-shaped line into a dark and a light segment, representing respectively yin and yang, each containing a "seed" of the other.

**ying ch'ing** (**Ying Ch'ing**, **Ying ch'ing**)

A type of glazed porcelain produced in Jiangxi and other provinces, chiefly during the Song dynasty.

**Yu**

An ancient Chinese wine vessel in the form of a small metal pail with a swing handle and a decorative cover, popular in the Shang and Early Zhou periods.

**yuan hsiao**

A sweet rice-flour dumpling made for the Chinese Lantern Festival (15 January in the lunar calendar).

**yüeh** (**yueh**)

A bronze battle-axe or halberd, esp. one of the Shang period.

**yüeh ch'in** (**yueh-ch'in**, **yu-kin**, **yukin**, **yu' kin**)

A Chinese lute with four strings and a flat, circular body.

**yulo** (**yuloh**, **yulow**)

A Chinese sculling oar.

Also as *v.* intr. to scull a boat with such an oar.

## 4.4 Summary

"No dictionary could ever list all English words, since the vocabulary is almost infinitely extendible by regular processes of word formation as well as by borrowing from other languages." (Durkin, 2014: 23) No sole dictionary can be an absolute authority. Dictionaries have their own purpose and scope, which determines what information to include or exclude. Language is in constant change, thus making dictionaries outdated in a few years; hence the need for frequent revisions. It is important to remember that a dictionary need not define all words and record all printed occurrences of a word; the illustrative sentences are a selection for purely illustrative purposes. This is the reason why it is important to consult sources other than dictionaries in the study of words, and especially of loanwords.

# Chapter 5 Chinese Loanwords in the Context of World English

## 5.1 Introduction

To attain a global status, a language needs to fulfill at least two requirements. First it should receive due official recognition within the international community. According to Crystal (2003: 3), a language achieves global status when it develops a special role that is recognized in every country. This special status can be achieved either by making it an official language of the country or by requiring it to be studied as a foreign language. Second it needs an expanding number of non-native users.

English, the first acclaimed global language, had massive contact with other languages in the 19th century as a result of British colonial imperialism and continued its global presence when America emerged to become the superpower by the end of the 20th century. Modern technology has turned the world into a small village. The Internet can carry English, the world language, to every corner of the world. The current spread, scope and scale of English is unprecedented. At the start of the 21st century, English is the main language of books, newspapers, international business, academic conferences, science, technology, medicine and diplomacy, to mention just a few examples (Crystal, 2003). In addition, English has official or special status in over 70 countries, covering Africa, Asia and the Pacific. English has become a globalizing medium, influencing language, communication and even culture all around the world. That means English has more sources to take in vocabulary. During the interaction between English and languages all over the world, more and more words of foreign origins will enlarge English vocabulary and increase its expressiveness. The wider the range of English use the more likely it will absorb foreign words.

According to the estimate by the Global Language Monitor, the number of words in the English language is 1,035,877 on January 1, 2016. Currently there is a new word created every 98 minutes or about 14.7 words per day. In this World English context, with the closer ties between China and English speaking countries, words of Chinese origins are making greater contributions to the English vocabulary.

## 5.2 World English

English has shown a remarkable expansion in its number of speakers and in their global geographical spread (Durkin, 2014:

303). English is currently the most widely spoken language in the world. If the number of speakers of English includes speakers of pidgins and creoles as well as speakers of English as a foreign language, Crystal (2003: 69) estimates that roughly 1.5 billion people speak English. Mandarin Chinese may have more speakers, but no language is spoken in more parts of the world than the English language. The global reach of English is one reason the language has more non-native speakers than native speakers. The popularity of English has a lot to do with geopolitical considerations: the initial spread of English worldwide as a consequence of British colonization, and the rise in the 20th century of the United States as an economic and political power in the world. Although American and British are the two major national varieties of the language, with the largest numbers of speakers and the greatest impact worldwide, there are many other varieties of English used around the globe. Today English is used as a first language, as a second language, and as a foreign language. Other important first-language varieties of English are those of Australia, Canada, Ireland, New Zealand, and South Africa. English is extremely important as a second language in India and has official or semi-official use in the Philippines, Malaysia, Tanzania, Kenya, Nigeria, Liberia, and other countries in Africa, the Caribbean, the Pacific, and elsewhere. It is the international language of the airlines, of the sea and shipping, of computer technology, of science, and indeed of communication generally. In the course of its spread, English has diversified by adapting to local circumstances and cultures, so there are different varieties of English in every country (Algeo, 2010: 199).

The conceptualization of the term "World Englishes" is within a "socially realistic" approach to language study (Kachru, 2006). The past decade has seen an unprecedented growth in the study of world Englishes (Mullany & Stockwell, 2010). It is a field which has grown rapidly since the early 1980s, reflecting the spread of English as an international language. The expansion of different varieties of Englishes around the world has been intensified by English as the global language of the Internet and therefore the dominant form of all different types of computer-mediated communication. The term World Englishes can thus legitimately be seen as a sub-disciplinary area of English language enquiry in its own right.

Braj Kachru (1986) produced a framework for conceptualizing World Englishes. Kachru argued that instead of thinking about "English" in singular form, the language should be seen as a pluralized concept. The whole range of different types of Englishes around the world should be perceived as belonging within one of three concentric circles, which he termed the Inner, Outer and Expanding circles. The Inner Circle refers to the UK, Canada, the U. S., New Zealand and Australia, where the English language has its linguistic basis and where it is associated with longevity, tradition and culture. This inner circle loosely corresponds with the acronym ENL, English as a Native Language. The Outer Circle refers to contexts where English has become an official language due to colonization, which Kachru maps onto the category of ESL: English as a Second Language. Examples of this include Nigeria, Singapore, Malaysia and India. Finally, the Expanding Circle refers to situations where English is used as a foreign language, commonly referred to as EFL contexts. According to Diane Davies (2013), recent research suggests that some countries in the Expanding Circle have begun to develop distinctive ways of using English, with the result that the language has an increasingly important functional range in these countries and is also a marker of identity in some contexts. The use of English in China is one prototypical example of the third circle.

Similarly, McArthur (1992) discusses "English languages" with a diagram called "The circle of World English" (see Figure 5.1). The central circle implies a "world" or "international" English, which English speakers with differing national Englishes use with each other when they meet at conferences, business meetings, or on holiday. Crystal (1995) disputes whether such a variety yet exists. As far as vocabulary is concerned, it would not be clear, for example, whether car or automobile would be the preferred term. Nevertheless, Crystal agrees that when we meet English speakers from different national backgrounds, we take care not to use words that we perceive as peculiar to our variety; at the least, we check that our interlocutor has understood a word that we are not sure that they know. The languages inside the segments of the larger circle in McArthur's diagram are the national and regional standards of English. Outside the circle are the regional varieties (languages and dialects) of these standards (Jackson & Amvela, 2007: 121).

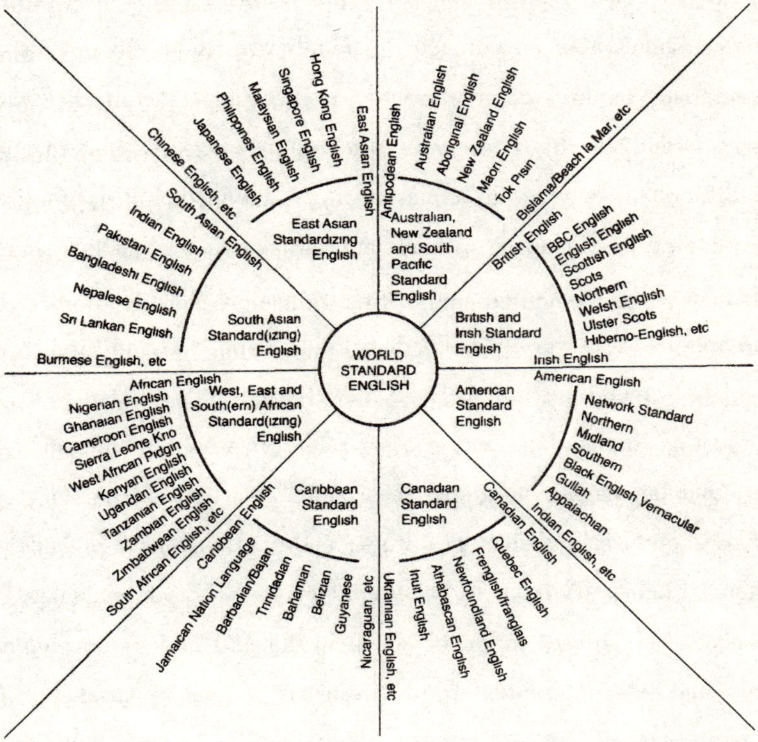


Figure 5.1 The circle of World English (McArthur, 1987)

Examples of English fulfilling the role of a lingua franca can be found in various locations around the globe. For example, English functions as the language of business, government, and the mass media in many African countries. Across Asia, English operates as a lingua franca in numerous countries, including Malaysia, Singapore, Thailand, and Indonesia. Barbara Seidlhofer (2004) reports that the majority of interactions which take place globally in English do not involve native speakers and thus English is being moulded and developed by non-native speakers just as much as it is by native speakers. For instance, native speakers of American or British English, who have extensive encounters with the users of Asian and African varieties should be encouraged to familiarize themselves with the characteristic features of appropriate varieties, and should show some awareness and sensitivity towards the repertoire range of other varieties. It is difficult to imagine an expatriate to be linguistically comfortable, for example, in Singapore without familiarity with the basilect and its users, and the interactional and creative use of such varieties. The same applies to the varieties of Indian English and Nigerian English and that of fast emerging Chinese English (Kachru, 2005: 131).

Just as English has, in the past, pulled in whole bundles of words from other languages, its global incarnation is set to do the same. As new speakers use English in new ways, and to talk about unprecedented matters, English is likely to be altered by an array of languages that haven't had significant influences on it in the past and its development is less and less determined by the usage of its native speakers. The diasporic communities—Chinese, South Asian, and others—are already altering the linguistic and cultural ecology of the Inner Circle. English has not only had a great influence on many other languages, but has also absorbed new words from such languages. "Given the demands and opportunities that are sure to face Earth's population in coming generations, we can expect the World English lexicon to explode in areas addressing critical spheres of common planetary concern such as communications, technology, education, health, migration, human rights, law, finance, climate change, security, and perhaps most vitally in coming decades, new sources of energy." (Dunton-Downer, 2010: 248)

New words continue to be borrowed as new things or concepts are encountered, or as a result of the particular prestige of a certain foreign-language culture in a particular sphere; if a new thing or concept becomes central to daily life, a borrowed word may also become commonplace, for instance *potato*, *tomato* (both from South American languages via other European languages), or today even *sushi* (from Japanese) in many English-speaking communities (Durkin, 2014: 302). Assimilation into a language as widespread as English occurs on three levels: local, national, and international. For example, such a Mexican-Spanish word as *taco* may remain local in American English, used only along the US-Mexican border, then become national, then international. Such a process often takes years, leaving many loans drifting uncertainly (McArthur, 1992). A word may occur very early in one variety, but take much longer to spread to other varieties, or it may stay regionally restricted for all of its life in English. It may even ultimately become obsolete without ever achieving any general currency. Numerous loans from a variety of languages reinforce the role of global language of English.

## 5.3 China English

The world has been made much smaller through technological advances. Contact between peoples and languages has become much easier. Seargeant (2005: 314) uses the term "globalization", coined to refer to situations in which "global pressures are made to conform to local conditions". Kachru (2005) has made a distinction between "genetic nativeness" and "functional nativeness". The degree of functional nativeness in terms of range and depth in a culture is an indicator of the dynamics of the English language and its changing profile. The more the range and depth of functions of English increase, the more distinct identities the English language acquires.

As China is opening up to the world, the language and cultural contacts with other nations are increasing, the Chinese people are experiencing a change in their language as well as their cultural outlook and are much more ready to accept foreign cultures and promote exchanges with other cultures in various aspects of social life. Chinese speakers have their significant participation in global exchanges, such as in financial sectors, manufacturing, technology, and cultural promotion. Chinese-speakers provide impetus for English to expand its vocabulary. China has the largest English learning and using population. It is estimated that there are 440-650 million English learners and users in China (Crystal, 2008). The learning and teaching of English has been an integral part of China's reform and modernization. English has been widely accepted as a utilitarian tool for science, technology, national development and modernization, and the study of English is regarded as necessary for acquiring technological expertise from abroad and for fostering international trade. The study of English in China is an educational industry as well as a national passion, pursued by millions of Chinese within the public education system and in private language schools. Apart from benefiting the entire nation in terms of scientific, technological and economic development, English language proficiency also has benefits on an individual level. Knowledge of English makes it easier to enter and graduate from university, travel or work overseas and get a better job, especially in joint ventures and companies involved in international trade.

English now has a higher status in China and is used more than at any other time in the past. Several investigations suggested that China English should stand alongside British English, American English, and other World Englishes. Although the terms "China English" and "Chinese English" are often used interchangeably, distinctions are often drawn between them. Chinese English or Chinglish (a blend of the words Chinese and English) tends to be used in a humorous or derogatory fashion to characterize English texts (such as road signs and menus) that have been translated literally and often imprecisely from the Chinese. Chinglish is sometimes characterized as an interlanguage. On a theoretical level, China English is distinguished systematically from Chinese English, Chinglish, Pidgin English, etc. China English is understood as a standardizing or standardized variety in use in China, which reflects Chinese cultural norms and concepts. China English is a language which is as good a communicative tool as the standard English, and it has distinctive Chinese characteristics and serves a variety of communicative, social and political purposes. It has spread both in China and outside China. Granted, it is still not on a level with other Asian Englishes such as Indian English and Singaporean English. China English is becoming a new variety that maintains high intelligibility in the global context and incorporates rich local linguistic and cultural characteristics.

Chinese students are among the largest communities in the universities of the US, the UK, Canada, Australia, etc. Chinese tourists are a common sight in many places of the world. Chinese academics regularly visit the West for conferences, and Chinese businessmen do deals on six continents. China's recent emergence as the world's fastest growing marketplace will undoubtedly influence the amount of contact English has with Chinese languages and the manner in which contact develops. In the United States and other English speaking countries, Chinese and things Chinese enjoyed great receptiveness, which promoted the lexical borrowing to some extent. The words borrowed into English, whether they are integrated or newly introduced, have constituted the unique features of China English.

## 5.4 Chinese Loanwords in Use

When we talk about words entering the English vocabulary, we are aware of the problem of determining stages of integration (Chan & Kwok, 1985: viii). When does a new word come fully assimilated into the English vocabulary? What criteria could be used to determine whether a word is part of the language or whether it is still "foreign"? The problem of assimilation is not an either/or matter, but there are intermediate stages(Chan & Kwok, 1985: 71). The idea of integration into English today is no longer one of "Anglicization" because of the existence of English as a world language. And the problem of assimilation is not a matter. Many Chinese loanwords appear in English mainstream media for the purpose of achieving accuracy, conciseness or effectiveness. In the following sections, we'll examine the widely used words of Chinese origin.

### 5.4.1 Familiarization of Chinese Loanwords by Native Speakers

Liang (2006) conducted a survey at London and Hong Kong respectively, showing that some words familiar to Hong Kong residents such as *Ching-ming*, *laisee* and *jetso* are unknown to British people. British people know quite well about some tea names, such as *bohea* and *hyson*, which are not frequently used by Hong Kong people. 70 percent of both parties know the following words *tea*, *wok*, *dim sum*, *litchi*, *chow mein*. Other words including *silk*, *mahjong*, *fengshui*, *yin and yang* are also well acknowledged.

Taking advantages of the convenience of the Internet, I conducted a small-scale survey in June 2014, by means of the online survey tool Survey Monkey. 156 people of various ethnic, educational and professional backgrounds in Connecticut, USA, provided their answers to a questionnaire concerning their familiarity of certain Chinese loanwords.

The following are some much recognized words arranged in the sequence from the most chosen to the least ones.

*Kung fu*, *Yin and Yang*, *chow mein*, *spring roll*, *mandarin*, *dragon boat*, *typhoon*, *feng shui*, *chop suey*, *wonton*, *Taoism*, *Tai chi chuan*, *dim sum*, *ginseng*, *Mahjong*, *wok*, *pak-choi*, *gung ho*, *kowtow*, *chow fan*, *nien hao*, *shih-tzu*, *Taipan*, *hong*, *cha*, *kuomintang*, *sampan*, *loquat*, *oolong*, *cheongsam*, *mao tai*, *hoisin*, *yamen*, *ding ho*, *chin-chin*, *kan pei*, *erh hu*, *kiang* (*jiang*), *cumshaw*, *k'ai shu*, *souchong*, *Renminbi*, *qinghaosu*, *kaolin*, *pai-hua*, *Maoism*, *Confucius Institute*.

One thing that these words have in common is that not all English speakers will know them. Although some words are easily understood by English-speakers, they are often considered to be "foreign" when the objects or ideas they refer to are not a part of their life and seems quite alien. Lack of interest in assimilating some aspects of Chinese culture is also a factor. Bloomfield (1933: 446) has written, "Cultural borrowing of speech-forms is ordinarily mutual. It is one-sided only to the extent that one nation has more to give than the other."

Another reason that explains the lack of familiarity of Chinese loanwords is the absence of a sizable group of English-speakers who know any Chinese. In order for large-scale borrowing to take place a considerable group of bilinguals has to be assumed. As a matter of fact, the vast majority of those who have any degree of bilingual mastery of Chinese and English are in fact Chinese. English-speaker would feel difficult to directly borrow the words when there is ever a need to describe Chinese customs, artefacts, and other Chinese things. This is highly associated with the disparate nature of the two languages. Unlike related languages such as, for example, French and German, the structures of English and Chinese are very different, and this tends to discourage borrowing and assimilation. Thus linguistic adjustments must be made before a Chinese word can become a fully assimilated member of the English vocabulary.

It should be noted that not all loanwords from a particular source language are of similar importance in the vocabulary of English. For instance, the majority of the words that figure in the huge total of English loanwords from Latin are of relatively rare occurrence, but some occur very frequently, and have an important role in the language of everyday discourse (Durkin, 2014). It is the same case for Chinese words.

Surprisingly, informants can recognize some newly appeared Chinese words. It could be contributed to the modern ways of communication. For example, the word *Renminbi*, referring to the currency used in China is becoming more familiar to the English-speaking community through international trade and travel.

However, the informants' choices might not be representative since the sample of this survey is rather small. In addition, the mastery of vocabulary varies from person to person. The familiarity with the words and the objects designated by the words can only serve as a reference point rather than the sole yardstick for studying the words.

### 5.4.2 Semantic Fields of Chinese Loanwords

English speakers tend to borrow words from semantic fields that reflect the nature of the contact between the two cultures. Scholars usually explain that the large number of Latin loanwords borrowed into Anglo-Saxon as religious terminology—words like *altar*, *chalice*, *litany*, or *mass*—reflect the importance of Roman Christianity in England during that period. Similarly, nautical terms borrowed from Dutch during the Early Modern English period—words such as *commodore*, *cruise*, *deck*, *reef*, or *yacht*—suggest that Dutch prominence in seafaring had a significant influence on English speakers (Moody, 1996: 405). When there is cultural borrowing, there is always the likelihood that the associated words may be borrowed too. Cultural borrowing of speech forms is originally mutual; that is to say, as far as cultural borrowing is concerned, all languages are equal and have the same chance to lend to, or borrow from, all or most of other languages, regardless of the cultural intimacy or topographical closeness between or among the languages (Hu, 2001:77). Cultural differences may have played a significant role in the lexical borrowing from Chinese to English. As Stockwell & Minkova (2001: 3) state, "English has usually borrowed words from other languages to get new words to cover new concepts or new material or abstract phenomenon. Words referring to notions and objects specific to other cultures are often borrowed wholesale." Semantic fields of Chinese loanwords are mainly words associated with Chinese cultural prominence. Although human experience cannot be divided neatly into compartments, for convenience of discussion, we put Chinese loanwords into a number of different semantic fields in the following sections. The discussion is illustrated with examples taken from a variety of different sources.

Vocabulary of Chinese food has contributed a lot to the whole bunch of loanwords to English. They are the earliest batch of Chinese vocabulary that entered English. Evidence of linguistic contact between English and Chinese can be found in records of Chinese foods in the West.

The basic food most closely connected with China in the Western mind is rice. Rice has been an important element in the Chinese diet for a long time. The importance of rice explains why a Chinese proverb states that "even a clever wife can't cook without rice". *Kaoliang* (sorghum) and millet are important food crops in north and northeast China. *Kaoliang* is also used as an animal feed and converted into alcohol for a beverage; the stalks are used to make paper and as a roofing material. Oats are important chiefly in Inner Mongolia and in the west, notably in Tibet.

Oilseeds play a major role in Chinese agriculture, supplying edible and industrial oils as well as other food products. The most important oilseed is the soybean, which is grown mainly in north and northeast

China. Chinese soybeans are particularly good for making *tofu* (bean curd), and the oil made from soybeans is used in cooking. *Soy sauce* is made by fermenting a mixture of soya beans, flour, salt and strains of fungi. *Soy sauce* is defined in Collins as "a dark brown liquid made from soya beans and used as a flavouring, especially in Chinese cooking". Black bean sauce was originally made from boiled soya beans which were then fermented with a fungus. Other important oilseed crops are sesame seeds, sunflower seeds, and rapeseed. The seeds from the fruit of the *tung* tree also provide a valuable oil, which is used as an additive in paints and varnishes. More than half the *tung oil* produced in China originates in Sichuan. The term *tung oil* is recorded in mainstream English dictionaries, such as OED, Collins and Random House.

Chinese food, taken as a whole, uses a very wide selection of vegetables. In the context of Western acceptance of Chinese food, however, only some of these have a particular significance. The vegetable known as *bok choy* (or *pak choy*, *pak choi*) also goes under the name of Chinese cabbage. *Bok choy*, which reflects the Cantonese pronunciation, has gained entry into American English. The Online Etymology Dictionary defines it as "type of Chinese cabbage, from Cantonese, literally 'white vegetable'."

Other vegetables identified as Chinese food include *water chestnuts* (known in China as *mati* or *biqi*), bamboo shoots and lotus root. In Chinese cookery books, four other plants used in Chinese food may be mentioned: the lotus, the lily, seaweed and varieties of fungi. Lotus leaves are used to wrap food and the lotus root is commonly used around Guangzhou as a food medicine, said to promote fertility. Lily buds, known otherwise as *golden needles*, which have an unusual musty taste, are used in some meat dishes. Several varieties of seaweed are eaten, including the red algae called purple laver. As for fungi, three of the most common used in Chinese cooking are padi-straw mushrooms, and those known as *wooden ear* and *monkey head*. *Wooden ear* is a type of bracket mushroom which grows on fallen trees. *Monkey head*, also known as hedgehog fungus because of its strange appearance, is a delicacy found in the forests of the northeast. *Ginger*, although not native to China, was already known in Zhou times and has since been widely cultivated. *Five-spice powder*, a combination of star anise, fennel, cinnamon, cloves, ginger and cardamom, is used to season red-cooked meats and poultry. *Ginseng* may be mentioned in this context, although it is used more as a medicine than as a spice or flavoring, for it is believed to add *qi* or vital essence.

Some fruit may be considered as Chinese food, the most typical being the *lychee* and the *longan*. The *lychee* was probably first domesticated in South China and it is now cultivated extensively in Guangdong. The word is variously spelt *lychee*, *litchi*, *lichee*, *leechee*, *liche*. The name is a phonetic borrowing from the Chinese 荔枝. The popularity of the fruit has led to its being imported into many Western countries and hence to the widespread currency of the term abroad. It may be worth comparing the relative currency of *lychee* and another phonetic loan naming a fruit indigenous to Asia, namely *loquat*. *Loquat* comes from Chinese 芦橘 and the term is included in many standard English dictionaries. Indeed the Chinese community do not usually refer to this fruit by the name 芦橘. Instead it is known generally as the 枇杷. Thus, even the Chinese name which has given rise to the loan is rarely used (Chan & Kwok, 1985: 138). *Longan*, literally meaning "dragon eyes", is a direct translation of 龙眼, for the stones of which are said to resemble the eyes of a dragon. It has a long history of cultivation in China.

As Chinese agriculture developed, styles of food were determined to a great degree by the natural resources available in certain parts of the country, thus the vastly different manners of cooking and the development of distinctive regional cuisines of China. These are usually defined as the northern cuisine, centered on Beijing and Shandong province, the eastern cuisine of Shanghai and the lower Yangzi valley, the western cuisine, in particular associated with Sichuan province, and the southern cuisine, often described as Cantonese, from Guangzhou. Sometimes the food of Fujian province, in the south-east, is considered to amount to a separate cuisine. The northern cuisine tends to use wheat or millet rather than rice—Beijing duck is traditionally served with pancakes made from wheat flour. Another northern dish, Mongolian hot-pot, indicates that mutton is more commonly eaten in the north. The eastern cuisine has a reputation for gourmet cooking, with red-cooked dishes and delicacies such as Nanjing pressed duck. Sichuan cooking is often spicy.

Particular mention should be made of the "four Chinese delicacies": *birds' nests*, *sharks' fins*, *bears' paws* and *sea cucumber*. *Birds' nests* are composed of nest cement, a form of salivary secretion from swiftlets which nest in caves in southeast Asia. Western travelers' reports suggest that the consumption of *birds' nests* only became common from the mid-15th century. *Birds' nests* are regarded as a strengthening food and as a medicine. *Sharks' fins*, which first gained favor in Song times, are obtained from tiger sharks and shark-like guitar fishes. *Bears' paws* have also been regarded as a delicacy in Europe. Nowadays the shortage of bears means that fortunately *bears' paws* rarely appear on a menu. The *sea cucumber* or sea slug, otherwise known as the trepang, is one of several varieties of Holothuria which are dried and used in combination with other seafoods. A delicacy which appears on the menu of important banquets, it is sometimes described as "sea ginseng" and is claimed to be a strengthening food.

One typical and traditional food eaten by Chinese needs to be mentioned is *jiaozi*. *Jiaozi*, a popular dumpling-like food, is eaten during the Chinese New Year and year round in the northern provinces. Its stuffing is made of vegetables, meat or both. The favorite stuffing is Chinese cabbage and ground pork, seasoned with green onion, ginger, soy and sesame oil. Use of vegetables is only limited by imagination, but the choice of meat confines to pork, mutton and beef, in that order. With limited syllables in the language, the Chinese play heavily into homophones. Since *jiaozi* sounds the same as "the juncture of the old and new years", having it then forebodes a happy beginning. They look like the golden ingots "yuanbao" used during the Ming Dynasty for money, so serving them is believed to bring prosperity. *Jiaozi* is significant to the Chinese New Year's Eve in north China as *niangao*, a cake of sweet rice to the south, both believed to bring good luck. In some places, people prefer to wrap a coin in one of the *jiaozi*. It is said that the lucky one who eats the *jiaozi* with the coin will have a wealthy year with good luck coming one after another. *Jiaozi* has become commercialized today, available as frozen food in supermarkets, delivered home by food trucks and served in restaurants.

Chinese people are famous cooks. There are many cooking methods employed, among which five are prominent: stir-frying, red-cooking, clear-simmering, steaming and cooking drunken foods. These cooking methods call for the use of a variety of tools and utensils. The most important tool is the knife or cleaver, which has a rectangular blade and a wooden or bamboo handle. Originally made of iron, it is now available in stainless steel. The blade of the cleaver is used for chopping and slicing, the back for pounding or crushing and the side to pick up food. Another indispensable utensil in the Chinese kitchen is the *wok*. The *wok*, which is typically made of cast iron, which conducts heat rapidly and evenly, is ideal for stir-frying, but can be used for many other forms of Chinese cooking. The term *wok* is a direct borrowing from Cantonese. Once English-speaking people, especially in the United States, Britain and Australia, started to borrow the round bottomed Chinese frying pan as an essential piece of equipment in Chinese cooking, they borrowed the name as well, and *wok* has been gaining currency ever since. In this case *wok* clearly has the advantage of economy and freshness, over and above "Chinese frying pan" or some other circumlocutory descriptive name.

*Huoguo* (hotpot) refers either to the utensil or the dish prepared with it. Made of red copper, a typical *huoguo* is a vessel with a shaft running through as a hearth and airway. A grate in the hearth holds the charcoal and drops the ashes to the base, where a door controls air intake. First recorded around the year 220, *huoguo* was a wintry royal delicacy of the Qing Dynasty. By the early 1900s, numerous styles had evolved. Today, charcoal is being replaced by electricity and natural gas, and a *huoguo* may be as simple as a pot of iron or steel. The method of cooking is the instant boiling (shuan) of meat, vegetables, seafood and other foodstuffs. Hotpot is very popular in winter times.

The cooked-food stall (or the *tai pai tong*) originally appeared in Hong Kong. *Tai pai tong* or *da pai dang* now has become very popular in many mainland cities. It has been a way of life for ordinary citizens to get together with friends.

As for eating implements, the most important are *kuaizi* (chopsticks), spoons and bowls. *Chopsticks* may be made of a variety of materials, the best being made of ivory, while those in everyday use are made of bamboo, and increasingly, of plastic. The use of *chopsticks* goes back to the Shang Dynasty and has acquired a deep cultural significance (Roberts, 2002).

The names of food and beverage items are in various stages of integration, but one term would seem to stand out as being perhaps the most integrated of all phonetic loans from Chinese—tea. The term is a standard entry in any dictionary of the English language. Originating in the Sichuan basin, *tea* or *cha* appeared during the Han Dynasty. Tea's flavor was first appreciated along the Yangzi basin and south of it; in the North, Buddhist monks, who noticed that drinking tea helped keep them awake during long periods of meditation, spread its use. Only in the late 18th century, with the publication of *The Classic of Tea* by Lu Yu, did the aesthetic cult associated with the drinking of tea begin to develop, and thereafter tea drinking became widespread in China. *The Classic of Tea*, which gave the elite precise instructions on how to enjoy the brew (an art that lives on in the Japanese tea ceremony). Tea is processed into five main forms: black or fermented tea, *oolong* semi-fermented tea, green or unfermented tea, scented teas such as jasmine tea, and brick tea. By the time of the Yuan Dynasty, tea drinking had spread to the lower classes, becoming one of the "seven necessities" (the others were fuel, rice, oil, salt, soy sauce, and vinegar) of everyday Chinese life. By the 17th century, when tea first appeared in Western Europe, tea had become the universal drink of China and one of the defining characteristics of its civilization. Tea was one of China's most important exports and the taste for it brought first the Dutch, then the English, and finally the Americans to trade at Guangzhou. *Teahouses* were particularly ubiquitous after the spread of tea drinking to every rank of Chinese society. All of them were important social centers where men, in particular, liked to gather to relax, sip tea, crunch on salted melon seeds, gossip, smoke their pipes, listen to singers or storytellers, and perhaps have a more substantial bite to eat. In some teahouses, patrons could order and savor rare and delicious teas; in others, mainly in the south and especially in Guangdong Province, the food predominated.

The one-time alternative term for tea, i. e. *cha* from the Cantonese pronunciation, has become fairly firmly established in the vocabulary of English. A compound, *yumcha* (or *yumchar*), literally means "to drink tea", is often heard in gatherings of expatriates. In fact it refers to a Cantonese repast in which tea drinking is an integral part. A translation loan would not do very well because it would not give the full meaning, since drinking tea is only part, though an essential part, of the *yumcha* ritual. A full description would mean clumsy circumlocution. This is probably also the case with the perhaps even better known phonetic loan *dim sum* from 点心, the name for the various tidbits served at *yumcha*. *Yumcha* is taken in the early morning or at lunch time, and *dim sum* or small tidbits are consumed along with the Chinese tea. In many restaurants in Hong Kong *dim sum* snacks and tea are available up to the late afternoon. The case of *yumcha* as a phonetic import gives a good example of borrowing of this type taking place because of need-filling coupled with economy of expression. The term *dim sum* is a phonetic loan based on Cantonese pronunciation. *Dim sums* are colorful, fragrant, tasty and shapely, and they meet the needs of every eater in every season. The ingredients are of high quality and plentiful, the style is novel and there are many varieties such as egg custard tarts, mini spring rolls, cakes, steamed buns, green peppers with shrimp filling, meat balls, fried or steamed dumplings filled with everything from roast pork to Chinese leeks, and other delicacies. The wrapping of rice flour dumplings is so thin that the ingredients can almost be seen. Another favorite wrapping is the lotus leaf, filled with steamed glutinous rice and a filling. "There is usually no ordering. Instead you choose from a wide assortment of snacks that the waiters or waitresses bring out on carts and trays. You may prefer not to take chicken's feet and duck's webbed feet in black bean sauce, but they are delicacies for the Chinese. It may take you several visits to different restaurants before you can taste all the varieties and determine your favorites. In big hotels in Hong Kong and the West, you may find Western variations. Dim sum is often used for get-togethers. A film entitled *Dim Sum* (1984) depicts three generations of a Chinese-American family living in San Francisco." (Davis, 2005: 207)

It is interesting to note that the one variety of *dim sum* which has gained fairly wide currency in the vocabulary of at least American English is *spring roll* which is a translation loan based on 春卷, literally "spring roll". The term is familiar to any English-speaking person who has some acquaintance with Chinese food (Chan & Kwok, 1985: 66). It is an example indicating how the original expression can be translated without necessitating laborious circumlocution.

*Wonton* is another widely known term. The principle behind the making of *wontons* is similar to that involved in the making of ravioli, but wontons are not ravioli, and to use the Italian loan to cover the Chinese concoction would mean lack of precision. OED defines it as a small round roll or pocket of dough containing a savoury filling, eaten alone (after being deep-fried) or boiled in soup (wonton soup). It is also included in the Webster Online, "a Chinese food made of dough that is filled with meat or vegetables and often served boiled in soup." Collins provides two definitions: "a dumpling filled with spiced minced pork, usually served in soup; soup containing such dumplings." For the second meaning, "*wonton soup*" is used in most cases.

Wine drinking is much enjoyed in China. There are many games that the Chinese play while they drink, guessing games and betting games, and the loser has to drink. A frequently heard word is *kan-pei*, meaning "to drink up".

Possibly the best-known of Chinese alcoholic beverages is *maotai*. It gained international currency through the media with Richard Nixon's first visit to China. So far it does not seem to have gained sufficient currency to be used in international publications without some kind of a gloss, e. g. "I finished off with (and was finished off by) a glass of *maotai*, the phenomenally lethal Chinese clear spirit" (Chan & Kwok, 1985: 142). Here is another quotation from *TriQuarterly*, a not-for-profit American literary magazine.

... All such requests had been refused before, and our Chinese hosts were somewhat startled to see them surfacing again. They had planned to exchange friendly toasts and pledges of future cooperation over Mao Tai, an absurdly strong drink consumed in great quantities at banquets, although you don't see people falling down drunk on the streets at night the way you do in Tokyo. I did no more than raise the tiny glass to my lips, letting a few drops of liquor burn my tongue with every toast. (*TriQuarterly*, 1996 winter, Issue 98)

In an article in *Time*, the context provides the general meaning, and no gloss is used. During an official visit to Peking in 1983 U. S. Vice President George Bush "lifted his glass of mao-tai at the banquet given in his honour" (Chan & Kwok, 1985: 142).

The meaning of the word *kaoliang* (*gaoliang*), in addition to the name of grain, equals Kaoliangjiu (literally "sorghum liquor"). It is a strong distilled liquor, made from fermented *gaoliang*.

Many traditional Chinese food terms are phonetic loans. While for dishes less familiar, a mixture of methods is used. Sometimes the straight descriptive names are used, such as *steamed beef balls* and *beef with oyster sauce*. Then they may resort to loan translation, possibly for the sake of giving a sense of the exotic; there are dishes like *Peking duck*, *Beggar's chicken*. These direct translations and descriptive names have become new additions to the vocabulary of Chinese food. The use of "Chinese" as a prefix is also not uncommon, for example *Chinese ravioli*, *Chinese mushrooms*, or *beef steak in Chinese style*.

Of the four aspects of material civilization which the Chinese consider basic: food, clothing, shelter and transport, food, as discussed above, is an area which has provided the largest number of loan words. When it comes to items of clothing, very few names have actually entered the English language despite the continuing influence of oriental fashions and fabrics on the West.

*Cheongsam*, the name of the traditional garment with high collar and side slits is probably the best known word in the category of clothing. *Cheongsam* (also known as *Qipao* or *Chipao*) is a traditional Chinese close-fitting dress for women. Its main characteristics are a mandarin collar, fitted waist, Chinese knotted buttons, hemmed slits on two sides, and a tailored form fit. It is usually made from satin brocade, silk, or cotton. Some are even beautifully embroidered. Collins defines it as "a straight dress, usually of silk or cotton, with a stand-up collar and a slit in one side of the skirt, worn by Chinese women". This dress had originally been the Manchu gown, known in Mandarin Chinese as the 旗袍 (banner gown), for the Manchus having been divided into different "banners" each with its own banner or flag. The Cantonese have another name for the same garment, 长衫 (literally "long gown"). *Cheongsam* is a phonetic loan that has gained worldwide recognition. The word can be found in literary works with Chinese setting or report on Chinese issues in English news media. Following are some examples:

> Transforming Ms. Cheung into the impeccably clad and coifed Mrs. Chan required more than four hours of daily preparation. In each scene she wears a different cheongsam—a form-fitting, classic Chinese dress—cut from vibrant floral or geometric fabrics (often imported from the West) that harmonize or clash with the décor's wallpaper and curtains or echo the more subtle patterns of rain on pavement. The dresses tell a story of Western influence and Eastern tradition, sensuality and reserve, restraint and vibrant expression. ("Setting His Tale of Love Found in a City Long Lost", *New York Times*, 2001/01/01)

> For a new house in Colorado, designed in 1999 by ARO, a New York

architectural company, Ms. Bright conceived and executed panels of sheer wool for a 35-foot-wide window with a mountain view that look more like a rolling mist than curtains. To further the effect, the curtain track was hidden inside the ceiling. The fabric is suspended on stainless steel rods that reflect like bits of sun in the windows. The curtains are slit at the bottom like cheongsam or Chinese hostess dresses, letting transom windows at the floor slip a breeze into the room without displacing the curtains. ("A Curtain Maker Who Challenges the View", *New York Times*, 2002/02/07)

Two words naming types of fabric known to the English-speaker have been borrowed from Chinese. Both *nankeen* and *shantung* derive from names of places in China, the first originating from Nanjing city, and the second from Shandong province. *The Oxford Dictionary of Etymology* has this to say about *nankeen*: "cotton cloth originally made at Nankin or Nanking, chief city of the province of Kiangsu, China." Collins defines it as "a hard-wearing buff-coloured cotton fabric, named after Nanking, China, where it originated". The word is not much used these days. This is in contrast to *shantung*, which seems to be still current. The word comes from Shandong, a province in Northern China, and has come to mean "a soft undressed Chinese silk (usually undyed)" (OED). Collins adds that *shantung* can also refer to "a cotton or rayon imitation of this". The Chinese name for the fabric is 山东绸 (shandong chou). It is still used for making clothes, though it seems less popular now.

When it comes to housing, furniture, appliances and decorative items for the home, we find few phonetic loans with any sort of currency. This is in contrast to the situation in Chinese where there are quite a number of words borrowed along with the Western household items they denote, e. g. the sideboard, the bar, the sofa. It would be fair to say that the West has adapted little of the household paraphernalia of the Chinese. But there are some phonetic loans especially in the field of the decorative arts. Since their first contacts with China, Europeans and Americans have admired its industrial arts. The early traders returned to their native countries with examples of porcelain, cloisonne, ivory, wood and jade carvings, embroideries and manufactured silk. Three words connected with the manufacture of porcelain have entered the English vocabulary, these being *kaolin*, *petuntse*, and *china*.

*Petuntse*, spelt sometimes as petunse or petuntze, comes from 白墩子 (bai dun zi). It refers to a white earth, consisting of pulverized granite, often used in combination with *kaolin* in the manufacture of Chinese porcelain. *Petuntse* occurs in the numerous books about Chinese porcelain intended mainly for the connoisseur, but can also be found in works for the general reader (Chan & Kwok, 1985: 186). Unlike *petuntse*, which is little known to the English-speaking world, *kaolin* has become almost completely assimilated into the English vocabulary. *Kaolin*, a fine clay produced by the decomposition of feldspar, is used in the manufacture of porcelain. The etymology given in OED is that it is from Chinese *kao* meaning "high" + *ling* meaning "hill", and that this is the name of a mountain in North China where *kaolin* was first obtained. Though *kaolin* was first employed by the Chinese it was subsequently found in many places. While most English speakers of some education know the term few are aware of its Chinese origin (Chan & Kwok, 1985: 187).

A much better-known loan word in the field of transport, indeed one recorded by most historians of the English vocabulary is *sampan*. This word is generally said to derive from the expression *san-pan*, meaning "three boards". The term has been in use since the early 17th century, referring to any small boat of Chinese pattern in the China seas. These boats were observed by early travellers to China. C. Toogood Downing describes the boats at the Chinese part of Whampoa in this way: "From some of the largest, let us now turn to one of the smallest boats at Whampoa. . . . you see a Chinaman. This is the barker. He is seated in the stern of a small san-pan, about ten feet long and just wide enough to hold his body while his legs are stretched forward towards the bow. The trim bark is just large enough to support him on the surface." (Chan & Kwok, 1985) The word *sampan* has been assimilated into the English language to a very high degree. It is recorded in standard dictionaries of British and American English. The written form is almost always unmarked. Its meaning now has expanded, referring to a small flat-bottomed boat (skiff) propelled by two oars or a single rear-mounted oar (scull). Look at the following example:

> Boat officers were given wide berth in "free-fire" zones where troops were allowed to shoot first and ask questions later. Kerry preferred caution unless fired upon. "He wouldn't let you go randomly down the river shooting up everything in sight," says Stephen Hatch, who served on the first of Kerry's two boats. Still, innocents were sometimes killed. One pitch-black night, Kerry's PCF-94 stopped a Vietnamese sampan boat after curfew in a free-fire zone. Kerry told his gunner to fire a warning round, but in the ensuing confusion the entire crew began shooting. ("John Kerry's Vietnam", *USA Today*, 2004/04/13)

*Typhoon*, even though its etymology is controversial, has attained complete integration into the English vocabulary. It referred to a phenomenon unique to the western Pacific area and the China seas, and traders must have encountered it from the time they first began to trade with China by sea (Chan & Kwok, 1985: 161). The OED suggests it is partly via Portuguese from Arabic *tufan* (perhaps from Greek tuphon "whirlwind" and reinforced by Chinese dialect *tai fung* "big wind").

A word closely associated with travel by sea is the verb *shanghai*, derived from the name of a city in China. The verb *shanghai* means "to kidnap (a man or seaman) for enforced service at sea, especially on a merchant ship" (Collins). Its origin is from the formerly widespread use of unscrupulous means to procure sailors for voyages to the Orient. The metaphorical extensions of meaning from this very compressed figurative use of a proper noun are multifarious in literary and non-literary use. This word can have its inflectional forms. Here is an example of its past tense:

> My spoken voice is wandering alone a dim room, rigor-seething with critical bent. That's zero fun. And here tonight we've been shanghaied, my wife and me, by my sister's logorrhea, in our resort's western bar and grill decored with hay bales, wagon wheels, sawdust. Slender rifles above a kiva fireplace the waiter assured my sister were cleaned and ready to fire. (*Western Humanities Review*, 2015, Vol. 69, Issue 1)

Apart from aspects of material civilization, the Chinese, as is well known, have a rich heritage of spiritual and cultural tradition. Chinese philosophy, religion, and social organization have many unique characteristics and names are required in English to refer to the characteristics and artefacts associated with these non-material aspects of civilization. The phonetic loans taken from the field of Chinese philosophy are, relatively speaking, fairly numerous (Chan & Kwok, 1985: 163).

The first complete translation of the Chinese classics into a European language is that of James Legge, an English Missionary. The classics consist of the *Four Books* and the *Five Canonical Works*. The title of one of these, known as the *I-Ching*, from 易经, or *Book of Changes*, is widely known in the West, although there are few who can claim to fully understand its contents. The original is written in enigmatic and symbolical language, and both Chinese and Western scholars have made various interpretations of the work. During the height of the hippy cult in the United States the *I-Ching* became a widely current work and the word has become fairly well established (Chan & Kwok, 1985: 163). Terms like *yin* and *yang*, in their phonetic loan forms had their semantic content loosened up and were used more generally. The pronunciation of the loan words is based on Putonghua. *Yin* refers to the female principle, while *yang* is the male principle in the universe. The Webster gives these definitions: "yin dark, feminine principle: the feminine and negative principle (as of passivity, depth, darkness, cold, wetness) in nature that according to traditional Chinese cosmology combines with its opposite yang to produce all that comes to be. Yang bright, masculine principle: the masculine and positive principle (as of activity, height, light, heat or dryness) in nature that, according to Chinese cosmology, combines and interacts with its opposite yin to produce everything that comes into existence." The ideas involved in understanding the working of these principles are complicated and philosophical. The borrowed forms *yin* and *yang* tend to be used with a degree of simplification, often simply to mean "female" and "male" respectively (Chan & Kwok, 1985: 164).

Another word which is current in the West is *fungshui* or *feng shui*, literally "wind and water". *Fengshui* is an ancient art form that deals with the placement of buildings or other structures so as to attain the most auspicious prospect. The present form of *fengshui* practice was probably started in the first century for the siting of graves and houses. The fundamental element of *fengshui* is the live spirit or energy circulating in the physical environment that can be captured and contained for the benefit of the inhabitants of the house, or the descendants of the deceased. *Fengshui* principles were widely practised by all sectors of the society even after the May Fourth Movement of 1919, when its practice was branded superstitious alongside other folk religions and practices. After 1949, it was regarded as one of the poisonous remnants of the old society and thus prohibited. In the meantime, *fengshui* practices continued to be widely observed in Hong Kong and Taiwan, fuelled by the economic prosperity of the 1980s. Similarly, with the economic liberalization of China since 1979, *fengshui* principles have again been applied, particularly in the business community. In bookstores books on *fengshui* principles can be found. Some books list simple rules of thumb for *fengshui* placement, such as the orientation of the frontdoor or furniture, while others start with first principles. With commercial activities increasing all over China, *fengshui* practitioners and literature will continue to be in great demand, and the proliferation of easy-to-use *fengshui* guides will allow more individuals to alter their living environment, usually just the furniture, in the hopes of a brighter future (Davis, 2005). In modern architecture, *fenghsui* is also taken into consideration. For example:

The Jin Mao Building, like the Petronas Towers, is eighty-eight stories

> high, eighty-eight being a lucky number in much of (Chinese) Asia. Fengshui characteristics are taken into consideration in building design, for modernism has not erased traditional worldviews. The 1,500-foot-tall Shanghai Financial Center, now under construction in Pudong, will soon eclipse the Jin Mao Building as the tallest structure not merely in China but in the world. (*Geographical Review*, Vol. 88, October, 1998)

There are three mythical animals unique to Chinese culture. The first two are known to the English-speaking world by the names "dragon" and "phoenix", sometimes with the prefix "Chinese" added, as in "the Chinese dragon". The last has given rise to the phonetic loan *kylin* or *ch'i-lin*, although sometimes it is referred to as "the Chinese unicorn".

Traditional Chinese medicine (also known as TCM) is a range of traditional medical practices originating in China that developed over several thousand years. The English phrase TCM was created in the 1950s in order to export Chinese medicine. In fact, TCM is a modern compilation of traditional Chinese medicine. TCM practices include theories, diagnosis and treatments such as herbal medicine, acupuncture and massage; often *qigong* is also strongly affiliated with TCM. TCM is a form of so-called Oriental medicine, which includes other traditional East Asian medical systems such as traditional Japanese and Korean medicine. Much of the philosophy of traditional Chinese medicine derived from the same philosophical bases that contributed to the development of Daoist philosophy, and reflects the classical Chinese belief that individual human experiences express causative principles effective in the environment at all scales. Following the macro philosophy of disease, traditional Chinese diagnostics are based on overall observation of human symptoms rather than "micro" level laboratory tests. There are four types of TCM diagnostic methods: observe (wang), hear and smell (wen), ask about background (wen) and touching (qie). The pulse-reading component of the touching examination is so important that Chinese patients may refer to going to the doctor as "Going to have my pulse felt".

Acupuncture and moxibustion constitute one of the most distinctive branches of Chinese medicine. Acupuncture refers to the therapeutic manipulation of needles at specific sites on the body, and moxibustion to the therapeutic warming or cauterizing of these sites with slow-burning moxa leaves. They are commonly used together in clinical practice, although acupuncture is the predominant technique. Acupuncture and moxibustion have a history of 2,500 years of practice in China and continue to be vibrant, evolving medical practices today. Acupuncture and moxibustion practice first emerged during the late Warring States and the early Han Dynasty eras. The oldest extant medical text in China, the *Yellow Emperor's Inner Canon* (Huangdi neijing), a collection of some of the most important medical writings of this period, devotes considerable space to expounding the basic principles of acupuncture and moxibustion. The innovations of subsequent generations of scholars have relied heavily on the theoretical foundations laid down in this classic. In contemporary practice, acupuncture doctors must master the basic theory of Chinese medicine, with a particular emphasis on meridian theory, acupoint location, and needle and moxa manipulation techniques (Davis, 2005).

Many westerners know of *Confucius*, the founder of *Confucianism*. *Confucius* was China's most famous teacher, philosopher, and political theorist, whose ideas have influenced the civilization of East Asia. The word *Confucius* comes from *Kongfuzi*, consisting of the surname *kong*, and a title *fuzi*, meaning "teacher" or "master". The name *Confucius* was first used by the Jesuits, and from this are formed *Confucian* as well as *Confucianism*. Confucius was a teacher from the state of Lu (in present-day Shandong Province) who lived in the 6th and 5th centuries BC. Confucius revered tradition and encouraged his disciples to master historical records, music, poetry, and ritual. He tried in vain to gain high office, traveling from state to state with his disciples in search of a ruler who would employ him. Confucius talked repeatedly of his vision of a more perfect society in which rulers and subjects, nobles and commoners, parents and children, and men and women would wholeheartedly accept the parts assigned to them, devoting themselves to their responsibilities to others. Confucius exalted virtues such as filial piety (reverent respect and obedience toward parents and grandparents), humanity (an unselfish concern for the welfare of others), integrity, and a sense of duty. He redefined the term *junzi* (gentleman) to mean a man of moral cultivation rather than a man of noble birth. He repeatedly urged his students to aspire to be gentlemen who pursue integrity and duty, rather than petty men who pursue personal gain. Confucius's teachings are known through the *Lunyu* (Analects), a collection of his conversations compiled by the succeeding generations of Confucius's disciples. Based primarily on the Master's sayings, preserved in both oral and written transmissions, it captures the Confucian spirit in form and content in the same way that the Platonic dialogues embody Socratic pedagogy. The eventual success of Confucian ideas owes much to Confucius's followers in the two centuries after his death, particularly to Mencius and Xunzi.

*Daoism*, also called *Taoism*, is an indigenous religio-philosophical tradition that has shaped Chinese life for more than 2,000 years. In the broadest sense, a Daoist attitude toward life can be seen in the accepting and yielding, the joyful and carefree sides of the Chinese character, an attitude that offsets and complements the moral and duty-conscious, austere and purposeful character ascribed to *Confucianism*. *Daoism* is also characterized by a positive, active attitude toward the occult and the metaphysical (theories on the nature of reality), whereas the agnostic, pragmatic Confucian tradition considers these issues of only marginal importance, although the reality of such issues is, by most Confucians, not denied. *Daoism* arose out of the promotion of *dao* (which means the way, or the path) as the social ideal. More strictly defined, *Daoism* includes: the ideas and attitudes peculiar to the *Daodejing*, the *Zhuangzi*, the *Liezi*, and related writings; the Daoist religion, which is concerned with the ritual worship of the *Dao*; and those who identify themselves as *Daoists*. The figure who stands behind all forms of *Daoism* is *Laozi*, who is traditionally regarded as the author of the classic text known as the *Laozi*, or the *Daodejing* (Kuiper, 2011: 90).

A third religion in China which is known to the west is *Buddhism*, or *Foism*. *Fo* derives from the Chinese word 佛 [fo] meaning "Buddha". *Fo* does not appear in OED, but is defined in Random House as "from Chinese, meaning Buddha." *Fo* is not a separate entry in Collins, but the abstract noun form *foism* is defined as "Chinese Buddhism, the version introduced from India from the fourth century AD onwards". We are told that foism is "from Mandarin Chinese fo

Buddha". We see that *fo* has entered the English language to the extent that it is used to form new words by the addition of traditional English affixes. Apart from fo-ism, there is also the adjectival and nominal form *foist* (Collins). The word *fo* appears in Romantic literature. In his Christmas letter (1815) to his friend Manning in Guangzhou, Charles Lamb complained of his long stay in China. In a mock burst of temper, he cries, "Down with the Pagodas—down with the idols—Ching-chong-fo and his foolish priesthood! Come out of Babylon, O my friend!" (Chan & Kwok, 1985: 168).

The Chinese lunar-solar calendar (*nongli* or *huangli*) is one of the few calendars in the world with a history dating back more than 2,000 years. It was first inscribed on bamboo slips and wooden strips in the third century AD, and from the 5th century onwards it was written on paper. Some traditional festivals such as *Spring Festival*, *Lantern Festival*, *Dragon-Boat Festival*, *Mid-Autumn Festival*, etc. are still celebrated by Chinese people at home and abroad. Some of the names of festivals are translation while others are loan translation.

*Spring Festival*, also called *Lunar New Year*, has more than 4,000 years of history. Being one of the traditional Chinese festivals, it is the grandest and the most important festival for Chinese people. It is also the time for the whole families to get together, which is similar with Christmas Day to the westerners. Originating during the Shang Dynasty (about 17th-11th century BC), Spring Festival, which celebrates family reunion, is full of rich and colorful activities, and hopes with the advent of spring and flowers blossoming. People from different regions and different ethnic groups celebrate it in their unique ways. It comes on the first day of Chinese lunar calendar and lasts for almost half of a month. But in folk custom, this traditional holiday lasts from the 23rd day of the twelfth month to the 15th day of the first month (*Lantern Festival*) in the lunar calendar. Among these days, the New Year's Eve and the first day of the New Year is the peak time. The exact days are different in every year according to the lunar calendar. Every family does a thorough house cleaning and purchases enough food, including fish, meat, roasted nuts and seeds, all kinds of candies and fruits, etc., for the festival period. Also, new clothes must be bought, especially for children. Red scrolls with complementary poetic couplets, one line on each side of the gate, are pasted at every gate. The Chinese character 福 (*Fu*) is pasted on the center of the door and paper-cut pictures adorn windows. On New Year's Day "well-wishing" (*bainian*) begins with worship of the gods, first the god of the earth, then the gods housed in temples. Only after the gods have been honoured can the visits to family and friends begin. The New Year is also the time when those families that have portraits of their ancestors hang them up above the domestic altar and when lineages worship together in the ancestral hall (*citang*).

*Yuanxiao Jie* is sometimes called *Lantern Festival*. In rural areas, the festival is often the highlight of the New Year Festival, with parades of lanterns that mark the reincorporation of households into their community. Some legends associated with the festival have romantic themes, and Chinese businesses have sought to present it as a kind of indigenous version of Valentine's Day. With its multiple levels of meaning encompassed within a single calendrical event, the *Lantern Festival* provides a rich example of the reinvention and transformation of tradition in contemporary Chinese popular culture. Dragon and lion dances, as well as in lantern processions and competitions are common activities during the Chinese New Year. *Kung Hei Fat Choy* , from 恭喜发财, is used as a greeting during Chinese New Year, during which period the expression appears frequently in the media and is also used among friends and acquaintances, both Chinese and expatriate. In Hong Kong English, there is a word *laisee*, from 利事, meaning "making matters propitious". It is used to refer to money given in small red envelopes to confer luck on the recipient, and sometimes goes under the descriptive name of "red packet" or "lucky money". The phonetic loan *laisee*, however, is current both in Hong Kong as well as various Chinatowns overseas. Most expatriates in Hong Kong have no trouble understanding the term, which occurs in conversation as well as in written texts, e. g. "Well-wishers brightened the Governor's day yesterday with get-well cards, laisees and a rose—not to mention four Bibles which Sir Murray did not accept because he already had one . . ." (Chan & Kwok, 1985: 170)

*Qing Ming* is one of the 24 solar terms in the traditional Chinese calendar, and usually described as a festival of the dead, which takes place fifteen days after the spring equinox. It is the time when winter is over, spring is on, the sky is clear and fields are green. Nature is full of vitality and ready for cultivation. That's why it is called *Qing Ming*, literally "clean and clear". It is a traditional Chinese holiday and the most important day for mourning, the time for worshipping ancestors and paying tribute to the deceased at their tombs which is called 扫墓, literally "to sweep graves". Sweeping graves implies more than just to clean and wash the tombstones and pluck the wild grass surrounding the graves, but includes other rites of respect (Chan & Kwok, 1985: 65).

Another transliterated name of festival is *Chong Yang* from 重阳 (literally, "double yang"), which falls on the 9th day of the 9th moon, or "double nine". Nine is considered a "yang" number by the Chinese.

For the *Duanwu Festival*, people make glutinous rice rolls (*Zongzi*) and hold dragon boat races. The traditional explanation of this festival is that these acts are performed in honour of the poet and patriot Qu Yuan, who, unjustly accused and banished, committed suicide by leaping into the river on that day. It is also generally recognized that the festival has an exorcistic function, inasmuch as people hang prophylactic plants on their doors. More explicitly, the dragon boat races are meant to drive away the gods who bring epidemics.

The 15th day of the 8th month in the Chinese lunar calendar is *Zhong Qiu Jie*, or the *Mid Autumn Festival*. It has many other names, such as *Qiu Xi* (the autumn night), *Ba Yue Jie* (the 8th lunar month festival), or *Ba Yue Ban* (mid 8th lunar month). It is the time of full moon, a symbol of family reunion, so it is called *Festival of Reunion*. All the activities of *Zhong Qiu Jie* being moon-related, it is also called the moon festival, night of the moon, the festival of chasing or worshiping the moon, etc. The common celebration activities are moon-watching and eating mooncakes (Davis, 2005).

When people have taken care of basic requirements such as food and shelter, they look for recreation and entertainment. The names of some of these pastimes, especially those associated with martial arts and sports have contributed to the phonetic loans taken into English (Chan & Kwok, 1985: 182). Two words, *Tai Chi* and *Kung Fu*, which have become familiar words to English-speakers, are from the field of Chinese martial arts.

*Tai chi chuan* (or *tai ji quan*), refers to a Chinese martial art and system of calisthenics, consisting of sequences of very slow controlled movements. *Tai chi* derives from 太极 or the "grand ultimate" in ancient Chinese philosophy. The *quan* means "fist" or less literally, some form of physical exercise. *Tai chi chuan* theory and practice evolved in agreement with many Chinese philosophical principles, including those of *Daoism* and *Confucianism*. *Tai chi* is based on the Chinese principle of *yin* and *yang*, in which opposing but complementary forces combine to create harmony in nature. According to traditional Chinese medicine, disease is caused by a disturbance in the flow of *qi* (chi), or life force. Practitioners of *tai chi* believe that it can promote physical health because it enhances the flow of *qi*. *Tai chi* is also taught as a form of meditation and mental exercise in which students learn to center and focus their mental powers. Many legends surround the origins of *tai chi*. One states that it was invented in the late 14th or early 15th century by Zhang Sanfeng, a wandering Daoist (Taoist) monk who had studied martial arts for many years. He observed a fight between a snake and a crane in which the snake won through relaxed, evasive movements and quick counterstrikes. Inspired by the snake's loose but controlled movements, Zhang Sanfeng devised a fighting form that emphasized strength, balance, flexibility, and speed. *Tai chi* is most commonly practiced as a series of movements known as the form. The form consists of a sequence of slow, carefully coordinated movements that flow together into one continuous motion. Individual movements have names such as "hand strums a lute", "part the wild horse's mane", and "the white crane spreads its wings". In its most advanced form, *tai chi* can be a powerful martial art. Over the centuries, *tai chi* has evolved into a system of exercise that utilizes soft, slow, relaxed movements. Today the most commonly taught basic form of *tai chi* is called Yang style, after Yang Luchan. *Tai chi* continues to be extremely popular in China, where in many places groups of people practice together at sunrise in city parks. "Tai Chi is an extremely popular form of exercise in present day Hong Kong. Tai Chi classes are given in many athletic clubs, and early every morning large numbers of people, some elderly, may be seen in parks and open spaces making slow, continuous, and rhythmic movements." (Chan & Kwok, 1985: 183) Today, *tai chi chuan* has spread worldwide and the health aspects are emphasized. It is practiced widely in the United States and other Western countries.

*Kung fu*, or *gung fu*, is used to refer to martial arts. Chinese people practice *kung fu* for the purpose of self-defense, and for health or other reasons. The Hong Kong *kung fu* master Bruce Li became an international star in the late 1970s, which helped to popularize the word as well as the art it refers to. One of the terms related to Chinese martial arts is *Shaolin*. Shaolin is from Shaolin Temple, a temple in Northern China where a group of masters trained their disciples in the art of *kung fu* of a special school. For well over a thousand years martial arts have been researched, systematized, developed and taught at Shaolin Temple. Shaolin training was a complex combination of para-religious health practices, exercises, lethal combat-oriented military methods and non-lethal self-defence methods. Because of its fame, Shaolin Temple attracted some of the most accomplished warriors and martial artists in China's history. There are records that indicate that Shaolin Temple in Henan province had been given the legal right to maintain a defensive force since the Tang dynasty. The early years of the Yuan dynasty were the most influential period for the development of wushu at Shaolin. Being associated with the Chinese chivalric tradition of heroism, *Kung fu* films (Wuxia films) produced in Hong Kong in 1980s were very popular in Chinese mainland. While the word *kung fu* has been borrowed in a Cantonese form (the transliteration is based on the Cantonese pronunciation), *shaolin* and *wuxia* are based on the Putonghua pronunciation (Chan & Kwok, 1985: 22). The *kung fu* related terms have gained recognition among *kung fu* enthusiasts in the English-speaking world. *Kung Fu Panda* (2008) and its sequel *Kung Fu Panda 2* (2011) are American computer-animated action comedy martial arts films produced by DreamWorks Animation. *Kung Fu Panda* premiered in the United States on June 6, 2008, and has since received favorable reviews from critics and much of the movie-going public. Kung Fu Panda opened in 4,114 theaters, grossing $ 20.3 million on its opening day and $ 60.2 million on its opening weekend, resulting in the number one position at the box office. The third installment called *Kung Fu Panda 3* made its debut in January 2016. Martial arts fiction (wuxia xiaoshuo) has been one of the most widely read thematic subgenres of mass-distributed popular fiction in modern and contemporary China, and the one most often perceived as expressing a uniquely Chinese sensibility. Wuxia xiaoshuo has been closely tied with similar material in other media, most notably martial arts films, and its themes, characters and imagery are well-nigh ubiquitous in Chinese popular culture.

The philosopher Confucius saw music and dance as enormously important to keeping society in good order, and both have always had an important role in Confucian practices. In imperial China, the ability to play and appreciate music was a central aspect of high social status. Although Chinese music has not made much of an impact on the West, the names of various traditional Chinese musical instruments are frequently mentioned when Chinese music is discussed. Two musical instruments are known to a proportion of expatriates by their translated Chinese names, these being the *pipa* and the *chin*, the Pinyin version of the latter being *qin*. Both *pipa* and *chin* ( *qin* ) occur in established dictionaries.

The *pipa* is a four-stringed, pear-shaped, fretted plucked lute from Central Asia that had appeared in China by the 7th century AD. Its body is made out of hollowed out teak covered with a soundboard of wutongwood. *Pipa* is defined in Webster as "a 4-stringed Chinese musical instrument plucked like a guitar and having a large body resembling a lute and a neck with 12 or more frets that leads into the body". Four strings traditionally made of silk ( now often of steel ) stretch from a string attachment and bridge located near the base of the resonator to their individual tuning pegs which are inserted two on each side of the head. A varying number of frets consisting of horizontal bamboo strips glued to the soundboard run from the midsection to the upper body and give way to frets consisting of triangular blocks made of ivory, cow horn or plastic on the neck of the instrument. The following example is taken from *Washington Post*.

> It was a wonderfully ferocious and illuminating performance nonetheless. Wu then took the stage (and shifted the tone) with Huiran Wang's delicate and light-filled "Dance of the Yi People" for solo pipa, which she brought off with effortless virtuosity. But this was all prelude to Liang's "Five Seasons", a sonic tour de force from a composer not yet 40. Full of rapturous invention, it unfolded with all the naturalness of a turning planet as it worked its way through the cycle of birth, death and renewal. The pipa and the quartet achieved a kind of exuberant synergy together, as if each were leapfrogging over the other in a mad rush to expressive extremes, and when it ended, it ended too soon. (*Washington Post*, 2011/02/28)

The *qin*, also called *guqin* (ancient qin), is a seven-stringed long zither without frets or bridge. The convex top of the *qin* is made of wutongwood and the flat bottom of ziwood (catalpa kaempferi), symbolic of heaven and earth, respectively. The strings are made of silk or silk-wrapped steel. The player plucks the strings with the right-hand fingers and stops the strings with the left-hand fingers. The three sounds produced—open, stopped and harmonics—represent earth, man and heaven, respectively. It is defined in Random House as a "Chinese zither consisting of an oblong, slightly curved wooden box over which are stretched strings that are stopped with one hand and plucked with the other". The *qin* is one of the oldest and most respected musical instruments in Chinese culture. Its history goes back three thousand years. It was the instrument par excellence of the ancient elite class, referred to in classical literature, and seen in landscape paintings again and again. It was also regarded as one of four types of knowledge necessary to the literati, the others being *qi* (chess), *shu* (calligraphy) and *hua* (brush painting) (Davis, 2005).

*Erhu* is the name used to refer to most Chinese two-stringed wooden bowed lutes with a slender neck that bores through a hexagonal resonator covered with snakeskin and a bow with the horsehair permanently inserted in between the instrument's two strings. These and similar type instruments used to be *huqin* in reference to their origin in areas beyond China's northern and western frontiers. It was only in the 20th century that it became a solo instrument. Sometimes, it is glossed or modified with Chinese when used in English language publications. Look at the following excerpts from *New York Times*.

> Many middle school students attend extra-credit courses after school or on Saturdays. A student at Jing'An, Zhou Han, 14, said she entered writing and speech-making competitions and studied the erhu, a Chinese classical instrument. She also has a math tutor. "I'm not really good at math," she said. "At first, my parents wanted me to take it, but now I want to do it." (*New York Times*, 2010/12/30)

> This (Mongols say) was the origin of the morin khuur, or horsehead fiddle, which in its travels along the Silk Road metamorphosed (musicologists say) into the Chinese erhu, the Persian kamancheh or spike fiddle, and all other bowed instruments of West and East, including Mr. Ma's cello. I have no idea what this story means, but never mind: I will twist it into a parable of imperialism. (*New York Times*, 2002/02/04)

The *di* or *dizi* is the name used today to refer to the Chinese transverse bamboo flute. It has six finger holes and, near the blowhole, an additional hole covered by a thin membrane which vibrates when the instrument is blown, resulting in a buzzy timbre. There are essentially two main types of *di*, each one a prominent instrument in the accompanying ensemble of two different opera traditions. One is the *kundi* (also known as *qudi*), which leads the instrumental ensemble of the *Kunqu* opera native to the area around Shanghai. The other is the shorter and higher-pitched *bangdi*, which figures in the ensemble of the Bangzi opera in Henan.

*Sheng* is a free reed wind instrument consisting of usually 17 bamboo pipes set in a small windchest into which a musician blows through a mouthpiece. Each pipe has a free reed, made of metal (or formerly of bamboo or reed), that vibrates to produce sound when a finger hole on the pipe is covered. Several instruments were derived from the sheng, including the Japanese sho and the Korean saenghwang.

While language is not the only part of culture, it is very important to culture. A language expresses the ideas, values and identity of its speakers. Furthermore, some aspects of culture are actually dependent on language. Songs, chants, stories and poems for example all depend on the phonological, morphological and syntactic aspects of language and without it they could not exist.

Interest in China and the Chinese has from very early times included an interest in their language. Although few English-speakers can claim to have any proficiency in Chinese, most are aware of the existence of numerous dialects and sub-dialects within the language. The standard language was *Mandarin*, originally known as 官话 (Guanhua) in Chinese, literally "officials' speech". It was used from the 16th century until the end of the Qing period. Mandarin Chinese is often non-technically regarded as an equivalent to Chinese, which was historically the language of the Han nationality. Thanks to massive immigration and frequent contact, Mandarin Chinese is spoken by non-

Han ethnic peoples as well. The word *Mandarin* was borrowed by the English-speaking world from Portuguese to refer to Chinese officials as well as the language they used. It is based on the dialect of *Peking* (Beijing), which was the capital of China throughout the period. In its broader sense, *Guanhua* refers to the language used in three-quarters of the land area and by over 70 percent of the population of China at that time. After the 1911 Revolution, the term was replaced by 国语 (Guoyu), literally "national language". It is defined as the language based on the everyday speech of an educated native speaker of the Peking dialect and the standard. It has the dual meaning of "standard spoken language" and "standard written language" although it refers mainly to speech and only to a lesser extent to writing (Chan & Kwok, 1985: 117). Immediately after the founding of the People's Republic of China in 1949, language reform was put high on the government's agenda. Modern Standard Chinese, officially called *Putonghua*, was adopted as the national language. It uses the Beijing dialect for its standard pronunciation and northern dialects as its base input. *Putonghua* is officially stipulated to be the language of instruction at all levels of education, and of mass media. The term *Guoyu* is still being used in Taiwan, while in Singapore it is called *Huayu* (i. e., Chinese). *Putonghua*, *Guoyu*, and *Huayu* are three different terms to refer to more or less the same Modern Standard Chinese (Gu, 2009: 215). As for the English-speaking community, the English term *Guoyu* meaning "National Language" never really caught on, and the two words they are familiar with are *Mandarin* and *Putonghua*, which they still use interchangeably in many contexts.

When a Chinese word is borrowed, it is written in letters of the

English alphabet. English speakers then pronounce the word according to the rules operating within their own language system. It is a fact that in the great majority of cases, the English speakers manage to pick up Chinese words by seeing their Anglicized forms printed in English publications rather than by hearing them spoken by Chinese people. To English-speakers the letters stand for English sounds. But the sounds of English and Chinese are not identical, and even if some may be very similar, they are apt to occur in different sequences relative to each other. This means that the pronunciation of the loan word would in many cases depart from that of the original.

There is a significant difference in the writing systems of English and Chinese. English has an alphabetic writing system while Chinese writing system is non-alphabetic. It applies a specific character to write each meaningful syllable or each non-meaningful syllable that is part of a polysyllabic word. Chinese writing is considered by most foreigners to be notoriously difficult to learn. Chinese characters have been evolving throughout recorded history, roughly from the "oracle bone script" (*jiaguwen*), through the "great seal script" (*dazhuan*), "small seal script" (*xiaozhuan*), and "clerks' script characters" (*lishu*), to the "regular script" (*kaishu*). Various cursive calligraphic styles, moreover, further abbreviated the strokes in the "regular script" (such as the running hand *xing*, and the cursive hand *cao*), which has lasted for about two thousand years and is still in use today.

Due to the push towards modernization a century ago, the Chinese language has undergone many reforms. As the earliest trade relations were with *Canton*, the English romanization accepted by usage has usually attempted to approximate the sound of the word in the *Cantonese* dialect. But the pronunciation of *Canton* is not that used by the majority of the Chinese people. It is necessary to standardize the system of transcribing Chinese words. Various romanization systems are used, such as the Wade-Giles system and the Yale system and the Barnett-Chao and Meyer-Wempe systems for *Cantonese*. Consistency and uniformity in spelling may be achieved after a time in the case of some loan words, while lack of standardization still characterizes a number of words in common use today. We have, for example, *kylin* or *ch'i-lin*, *lychee* or *litchi*, *tai chi ch'uan* or *tai chi chuan*, *wan tun* or *won ton*.

As a means of standardizing the transcription of Chinese characters, the *Pinyin* method was created by the Chinese in the late 1950s and has been steadily modified. The term *Pinyin*, which literally means "to spell according to sound", has entered the English vocabulary. This system of spelling has been adopted for use by journals and books published on a world-wide basis. In 1977 Chinese government made a formal request to the United Nations (UN) to have the *Pinyin* method of romanization used to transliterate Chinese place names. Words like *Beijing*, *kongfu*, *taijiquan*, now appear in their new *Pinyin* forms. Both *Putonghua* and *Pinyin* appear in the international media are gaining wider and wider international currency. The International Organization for Standardization (ISO) adopted *Pinyin* as an international standard in 1982.

### 5.4.3 Meaning Change of Loanwords

When a word or expression is borrowed it may undergo various changes in meaning. The borrowed item may become more general or narrower in meaning compared with the source item.

An example of a word becoming more general in meaning in the new language is *kung fu*. The term is now sometimes used as a modifier in *kung fu shoes*, which is used to describe a kind of soft cloth shoe with a flat sole and a strap which is buttoned down. In fact, this particular type of shoe is the traditional footwear for the Chinese, and is not used exclusively for doing *kung fu* (Chan & Kwok, 1985: 89)

We can observe the opposite process taking place in the case of *yin* and *yang*. In Chinese the two words stand for the male and female principles in the universe, and carry a mystical and rather abstract meaning. In English, however, the two words are sometimes made to carry a much narrower meaning, as shown for example in *The Noble House* where they are used to refer exclusively to the relationship between man and woman. For example, "You're strong and a man, yang, and I'm a woman, yin..." (Chan & Kwok, 1985: 89)

Another example illustrating the narrowing of meaning is the word *cheongsam*. When the Manchu ruled China during the Qing dynasty, certain social strata emerged. Among them were the Qi (Banners), mostly Manchu, who as a group were called *qiren* (Banner People). Manchu women typically wore a one-piece dress that retrospectively came to be known as the *qipao*. The generic term for both the male and the female forms of Manchu dress, essentially similar garments, was *changpao*, literally meaning "long jacket" and worn by both men and women, pronounced in Cantonese as *cheongsam*. Although it continued to be worn by some men after 1911 revolution, *cheongsam* refers usually to the rather tight-fitting garment with slits and Mandarin collar worn by women and the term *qipao* was more acknowledged.

The figurative meaning of *face* in the expressions *to lose face* or *to save face* covers a whole range of connotations: prestige, social acceptance, dignity, respect. The English-speaking world has evidently found it a useful term and the translation has found its way as a loan into the English lexicon. Indeed it seems to be so firmly established in the English vocabulary that the average native speaker is unaware of its Chinese origin. *The Shorter Oxford Dictionary* gives under *face* a definition of "to lose face" and gives in square brackets: [tr. Chinese tiu lien]. Under *save*, it gives "to avoid being disgraced or humiliated" as the definition of "to save one's face", and claims that the expression originated "in imitation of Chinese idioms". In *Webster's New World Dictionary*, the figurative definition of face is given as "self respect" or "prestige" and the Chinese origin is given. And indeed in most contexts there is little if any, sense of foreignness (Chan & Kwok, 1985: 60)

Occasionally, as a result of misunderstanding, the meaning of the borrowed term may lose its unfavourable connotations when it enters the target language. A case in point is the word *taipan*, now used to describe the top man in a large commercial organization, usually European-operated. It implies immense authority and power. However, the Chinese term was originally used to describe the "manager" of a group of dance hostesses working in a dance hall. In *The Noble House* we have this comment: "Very few Europeans knew that though tai-pan meant great leader, in the old days in China a tai-pan was the colloquial title of a man in charge of a whorehouse or public toilet." (Chan & Kwok, 1985: 91)

Some loanwords have been so integrated into English that they can produce new lexical items the same way as any native English word.

Such productivity is clear evidence that these loanwords have been fully integrated into English. The word mandarin has developed several compounds, for example, a *mandarin orange* is the fruit of a Chinese citrus tree; a *mandarin collar* is a narrow stand-up collar associated with Chinese-style clothing; and a *mandarin duck* is a crested Asian duck.

### 5.4.4 New Trend of Chinese Loanwords

Geographical closeness has been a very important factor in linguistics borrowing. It has been very difficult for languages geographically separated to borrow from each other, since in such circumstances they have few chances of getting into contact with each other. Nowadays, however, geography is no longer so decisive in linguistic contact. The forces of globalization are challenging the long existing close bond between language, territory and cultural identity, making a significant impact on the global use of a language. Languages and cultures are affected in communities by the inflow and outflow of people, images, ideas, technology and money. Modern communicative tools such as the Internet have made it easier for language users from all regions to overcome geographical barriers and come into frequent, wider and closer contact. Over time, it is possible that the regional varieties of a language will slowly go through a process of self-adjustment and is commonly accepted and widely used in the global community.

Globalization is not a linear process from West to East; the flow can be any direction. The English language is now open to new words on a worldwide basis. Dictionaries do not include some of the most recent loanwords. Words from another language are usually used to refer to things, patterns of behavior, organizations or ideas, for which there are no words or phrases in English to express or properly express.

Communication between China and the West dramatically increased; and consequently, the frequency of borrowing increased as well. Owing to the rapid development of modern mass media and international and cultural exchange, words that are related to Chinese society and culture have found their way into English, showing the changes in China.

China has already become the world's second-largest economy and is now one of the largest contributors to global growth. If China continues on its present growth track, it may soon take over from the United States as the world's largest economy. China has been exerting immense influence politically, economically, as well as linguistically, in the international arena. The economic and linguistic expansion of China has prompted many governments and non-governmental organizations around the world to realign their language perceptions and to recognize Chinese as a language of opportunity. The US government implemented a series of policies in favor of the teaching and learning of the language, including the "National Flagship Language Initiative", which classified Chinese as a "critical need language". "Chinese is widely believed to be the most likely candidate amongst the world's languages to attain the status of a language second only to English." (Seng & Lai, 2010: 15) The term *Duiwai Hanyü Jiaoxue* may be translated as "teaching Chinese to foreigners" or "teaching Chinese as a foreign language" (TCFL). The field has developed rapidly since China's reform and opening to the outside world. A large number of non-native learners undertake the "Chinese Language Proficiency Test" every year, showing the growing international status of Chinese. The Confucius Institutes set up all worldwide are making the Chinese language and culture teaching resources and services available to the world.

The rapid proliferating of Chinese language will provide more chances for the close interaction between Chinese and English. The new frontier for the spread of languages is not the national boundary but cyberspace. The Internet has an important supporting role to play in the global spread of Chinese language and culture. Chinese has the highest number of mother tongue speakers in the world. The Chinese are presently learning English. People in other cultures have become interested in learning Chinese and getting to know Chinese culture. Chinese has a potential to contribute more words in other languages, English in particular.

Because present-day English media extend far and wide, making borrowing of new terms and ideas both necessary and possible. Such temporarily adopted words are intended to stimulate the reader's interest and enhance the expressiveness of the reports. In articles in international journals about China today, it is not at all uncommon to find the insertion into the text of quite a number of Chinese terms and expressions written in *Pinyin*, sometimes preceded or followed by an explanatory gloss.

For instance, Tu Youyou's wining of the Nobel Prize in 2015 has brought about a hot word: *Qinghaosu*. It refers to a naturally occurring compound (also known as artemisinin) which is extracted from the Chinese plant Artemisia annua for use in the treatment of malaria. A direct borrowing from Chinese *qinghaosu*, itself derived from *qinghao*, the Chinese name for the Artemisia plant, and a suffix meaning "active principle". The plant grows alongside rivers in the North-East and South-West of China. The Chinese have known about the anti-malarial properties of the *qinghao* for many centuries—the leaves and stems are used in traditional Chinese medicine against fever—but it was not until the early seventies that these were confirmed by rigorous testing and identification of the active ingredient, *qinghaosu*. It proved effective against some types of malaria that are not treatable with synthetic anti-malarials. News of the discovery was reported in the West in the late 1970s and 1980s. Here is an example:

> One of the plants to come under scrutiny was a weed with a long history of use known in China as qinghao... The Chinese named the crystalline compound qinghaosu, meaning active principle, and the western version of the name is Artemisinin. (*The Times*, 1985/7/22)

The increasing use of Chinese *Pinyin* in English media can be illustrated by another word—*Gaokao*. *Gaokao* is the short term of "The National College Entrance Examination". This exam is given each summer and required for each student who would like to have their college education in China. The exam covers common school topics such as Chinese, math, English (or other foreign languages), history, science, etc. Better institutions require higher scores for admittance. The required score also varies by province: students in more competitive provinces need higher scores than students from less competitive areas. *Gaokao*, with its unique feature in Chinese testing system, has been playing an important role in promoting Chinese higher education and cultivating talents in every field. In the 20th century, when the admission number of colleges was relatively small, *gaokao* was regarded as a life-changing opportunity for young students. There was a saying that goes: *gaokao* is a fierce competition just as "thousands of soldiers and tens of thousands of horses across a single log bridge". As a consequence, in the background of exam-oriented education, teachers in middle schools tend to adopt the spoon-feeding method and students who have passed *gaokao* are not competent enough to solve practical problems. In other countries, similar tests, such as SAT (Scholastic Assessment Test) in the US and A-Levels (General Certificate of Education Advanced Level) in the UK, are also required for college candidates. People in western countries do not have so strong "feeling" for such exam because they have rational ideas for higher education and the educational resources are adequate. Recent years saw the dramatic increase in college enrollment, which make *gaokao* less competitive than before. Yet, in Chinese social life, *gaokao* is still a key issue for every family. Thus, at the "gaokao season" every year, social media always cover relative reports of the exam. Instead of using "college entrance examination", more and more overseas media tend to use the pinyin *gaokao* directly, sometimes with a parenthetical note.

In the following, we will take some excerpts from English newspapers or magazines concerning the report of the exam and discuss the use of this word.

(1) More than a million graduates took this year's Civil Service Exam—nearly twice as many as in 2006. At the same time, fewer high school students this year took the gaokao, the college entrance exam, thus turning their backs on the magic key that Chinese young people have always prized for unlocking the door to prosperity. ("China's Ant Tribe: millions of unemployed college grads", *Christian Science Monitor*, 2009/12/21)

(2) He believed an even bigger problem lay with China's intensely testbased

academics: a child's entire scholastic path—in some ways his or her life—could depend on one exam, the gaokao, the sole criterion for college entrance. The pressure was crushing; peers became competitors; teachers became slave drivers. Students had time only for rote memorization—not for singing or volleyball or after-school fun, otherwise defined. ("I Was a Chinese Internet Addict", *Harpers Magazine*, 2007 Mar, Vol. 314)

(3) Burnt-out and overtaxed, even kids who did well on the gao kao turn into virtual dropouts, choosing the respite of computer games over the university spots they worked so hard to win. Without a parent to push them, many stop going to class. ... Last January, for example, one 17-year-old Beijing girl tried to kill herself after learning that a paperwork snafu might prevent her from registering for the gao kao. Suicide has become China's fifth most common cause of death overall, with young urban intellectuals at highest risk. ("Plight of the Little Emperors", *Psychology Today*, 2008 Jul/Aug, Vol. 41)

(4) In contemporary times, strict and result-oriented parenting also has to do with anxieties created by a ubiquitous testing environment. In China, it is exacerbated by the one-child policy. The gaokao (college entrance exam), for example, has even been known to push students to suicide. ("Balancing Freedom With Discipline", *New York Times*, 2011/01/13)

(5) For the past year, Liu Qichao has focused on one thing, and only one thing: the gao kao, or the high test. ... China may be changing at head-twirling speed, but the ritual of the gao kao (pronounced gow kow) remains as immutable as chopsticks. One Chinese saying compares the exam to a stampede of "thousands of soldiers and tens of thousands of horses across a single log bridge". ("China's College Entry Test Is an Obsession", *New York Times*, 2009/06/13)

(6) But students from China can find themselves ill-prepared for the admissions process at American colleges. The education system in mainland China focuses on assiduous preparation for the national university entrance exam, the gaokao, often at the expense of extracurricular activities. ("Coaching and

Much More for Chinese Students Looking to U. S. ", *New York Times*, 2011/05/30)

(7) More than 9.1 million students throughout China sat for the college exam beginning Thursday morning, competing for 6.85 million places at Chinese universities, according to Ministry of Education figures reported by *China Daily*. The exam is known as the gao kao (高考), pronounced gow kow, and the number of high school test-takers has dropped each year since 2008, the ministry said, as the graduation-age population has decreased and more students gravitate to universities abroad. ... The gao kao remains, by far, the most important factor for admission to a mainland university. ("Putting Chinese Students to the Test", *New York Times*, 2012/06/07)

(8) Keju is dead now but its spirit is very alive in China today, in the form of gaokao, or the College Entrance Exam. It's the only exam that matters since it determines whether students can attend college and what kind of colleges they can attend. Because of its life-determining nature, gaokao has become the "baton" that conducts the whole education orchestra. Students, parents, teachers, school leaders and even local government officials all work together to get good scores. ... Chinese educators are well aware of the problems with the gaokao system and have been trying to move away from the excessive focus on testing. But seeking other valid indicators of strong academic records will take time, especially in a country of 1.3 billion people. ("High Test Scores, Low Ability", *New York Times*, 2010/12/02)

(9) China's annual college entrance exam, known as the gaokao(高考), took place this past weekend, affecting millions of Chinese students as well as the Olympic torch relay. According to Xinhua news agency, both the route and the timetable of the torch relay were adjusted on Sunday in order to minimize disturbance on the examinees in Baise, a city in southwestern China's Guangxi Zhuang Autonomous Region. ("How College Entrance Exams Shortened the Olympic Torch Relay", *New York Times*, 2008/06/11)

(10) In order to enter college, a student in Shanghai needed a score of at

least 412 on the gao kao. Wan's score is high enough to gain entrance to a vocational college, but he won't become a teacher that way. His options are to attend a vocational college or to wait another year and retake the gao kao next June. ("Judgement Day: A Shanghai Teenager Receives His Score", www. marketplace. org/topics/world/ [2013.05.09])

(11) My colleague in Beijing, Sharon LaFraniere, has written about the increasingly sophisticated cheating on the Chinese college-entrance exam, the gao kao, or the high test. ("Sneaking Into Class From China", *New York Times*, 2012/02/05)

(12) Students in China's test-centric culture spend most of their high school years studying for the gao kao, the college entrance exam that is the sole determining factor in whether students win a coveted spot at one of China's oversubscribed universities. ( "The China Conundrum", *New York Times*, 2011/11/06)

(13) In China, high school and the gaokao exam scores are the apex of many students' education. While the prestige of the university is very important for parents and students, the quality of education that a student receives at university is not always of the greatest concern. ("When Schools Officials Drive BMWs", *New York Times*, 2010/12/02)

From above examples, we can sum up the pattern of use of this word as follows:

1. gaokao appears as a proper noun, is always used with the definite article "the". The gaokao enjoys a very special status in China. It is a unique concept.

2. The spelling is not inconsistent. It is "gaokao" in examples as (1), (2), (4), (6), (8), (9), (13), while in (3), (5), (7), (10), (11), (12), it is spelt as "gao kao", which is regarded as a noun phrase. Gao, meaning "the high level", is used as a modifier. From the perspective of lexicalization, gaokao is still in its unstable

stage.

3. Examining the context where gaokao first appears, we can find different ways of its presentation.

a. explained by an appositive, as in example (1): "the gaokao, the college entrance exam".

b. followed by or plus an explanation, as in example (8): "gaokao, or the College Entrance Exam".

c. followed by an appositive clause, as in example (12): "the college entrance exam that is the sole determining factor in whether students win a coveted spot at one of China's oversubscribed universities".

d. followed by a parenthetical explanation, as in example (4): "The gaokao (college entrance exam)".

e. followed by a word indicating its category, as in example (13): "the gaokao exam".

f. preceded by an explanation, as in example (6): "the national university entrance exam, the gaokao", example (7): "The exam is known as the gao kao", example (9): "China's annual college entrance exam, known as the gaokao (高考)".

g. preceded and followed by an explanation, as in example (2): "one exam, the gaokao, the sole criterion for college entrance", example (11): "the Chinese college-entrance exam, the gao kao, or the high test".

h. used independently, as in example (3): "kids who did well on the gao kao turn into virtual dropouts", example (10): "a score of at least 412 on the gao kao".

i. followed by literal transition, as in example (5): "the gao kao, or the high test", example (11): "the Chinese college-entrance exam, the gao kao, or the high test".

j. followed by a note for pronunciation, as in example (5): "the ritual of the gao kao (pronounced gow kow)", example (7): "the gao kao (高考), pronounced gow kow".

k. followed by Chinese character in parenthesis, as in example (7): "The exam is known as the gao kao (高考)", example (9): "China's annual college entrance exam, known as the gaokao (高考)".

*Gaokao* could be regarded as a temporary loanword. It is likely to be more widely used and adopted into English vocabulary when more and more people get to know the exam. Whether it will become entrenched in the English vocabulary depends on time and other factors.

The use of the word *gaokao* may indicate some new trends of Chinese loanwords. Firstly, *Pinyin* has become the prior choice for transcribing Chinese words. Except for some established words which are spelled according to their Cantonese pronunciation by means of the Wade system, the newly introduced words are based on *Putonghua* and are expressed by *Pinyin* as a standard. The direct use of *Pinyin* will be concise, terse and maintain the cultural identity of the loanword.

Secondly, the range of loanwords became wider than before. Chinese words are not confined to food terms, and more words from the semantic field of economy, education, institution, etc. have become candidates of new loans. When people are concerned about a phenomenon or a concept, it is likely that the terms will frequently occur in press and increase its popularity. Like *gaokao*, other words that record the Chinese people's way of life, such as *guokao*, *jiayou*, *chunyun*, have gradually been exposed to a larger audience.

Thirdly, direct borrowing is becoming an alternative while explanations are still needed for certain loanwords. Before being massively used, some words should be accompanied with explanation or paraphrase either before or following the word so as to make its meaning clear to western readers. "When foreign words are used in English, it is natural for the writer to want to make sure that the words are understood by readers. Thus, in order to guarantee the foreign words are properly understood, they are often paraphrased with familiar and recognizable words." (Doi, 2014: 681) Chen (2012: 130) pointed out that during the promotion of local variety of English, we need do more to help other English speakers get to know the words with Chinese cultural connotations in the context through explanations and annotation. In time, if the word catches on, the italics, quotation marks, and explanatory notes may no longer be necessary. This certainly applies to a number of words occurring in publications. Many ways of explanation are used in the examples of *gaokao*. While in two examples, the word is used without any further notice. Even the Chinese character could be used, which is rarely seen in the past.

The mass media plays an important role nowadays in publicizing Chinese catchy words. English is open to absorb loans in a phonetic from. The following are some words expressed in Chinese *Pinyin*.

*Guanxi* (social relationship/social connections) refers to a whole complex of social practices, strategies and ethics of the exchange and reciprocity of gifts, favors and banquets. The social practice of *guanxi* seems to be a taken-for-granted part of everyday life. *Guanxixue* (the art of *guanxi* or *Guanxiology*) is what one needs to learn in order to conduct oneself appropriately in social relations, live up to obligations to one's circle of kin, friends, superiors and acquaintances, and also to enhance one's chances in life, obtain hard-to-find goods or get around the bureaucracy. While *guanxi* had evident roots in traditional Chinese culture, with its emphasis on proper Confucian ritual form, on kinship obligations, and on principles of *renqing* (human feeling) and reciprocity. *Guanxi* in some contexts is derogatory in meaning and becomes synonymous with corruption when some people break the spirit of fair play.

*Weibo* is a short term for Microblog. Akin to a hybrid of Twitter and Facebook, it is one of the most popular online social media in China. Sina Weibo has the largest number of users. There are other Chinese microblogging or weibo services including Tencent Weibo, Sohu Weibo, and NetEase Weibo.

Chinese *Dama* refers to a group of Chinese middle-aged women who rushed to purchase gold as an investment in the year 2013 when the gold price plunged greatly, especially in April and October. Due to the unpredictability in the rising and falling global gold market, Chinese *Dama*'s blind investments in gold may risk a lot. *Dama* generally represents a group of women that are deeply influenced by Chinese tradition, willing to serve within the household, and care about daily expenses. The *Pinyin* word *Dama* took on a new connotation, referring to a specific group of people, who panic purchase things, and it may also refer to the "rush to purchase" phenomenon.

*Tuhao* is a term with teasing tone, referring to those who are rich in money but not in class. The term has become popular these days with the unveiling of Apple's new gold-colored iPhone, which some consider gaudy. The *tuhao* are often eager to flaunt their new wealth. They buy fine clothing and accessories and fancy automobiles, and even purchase large, single-family dwellings near new private schools. Fancy restaurants, discos, and nightclubs are trendy venues for the newly rich to show off their wealth and status and enjoy a sophisticated lifestyle.

Some words are coined according to the rules of English word formation or translated literally from Chinese into English. These words will become widely known when being spread over the Internet. The following are some "hot words" in recent years.

The word *taikonaut* refers to a Chinese astronaut. It is a blending word based on the analogy of astronaut and cosmonaut. *Taikon*, in Chinese *Pinyin*, means "sky". Here is one example:

> Russia's Soyuz capsule, China's roomier Shenzhou V, or "Divine Vessel", spacecraft will climb into orbit atop a Long March 2 rocket and descend with its passengers by parachute onto the grasslands of Inner Mongolia, following the pattern established during four unmanned flight tests from the Jiuquan Space Center. At least some members of China's small taikonaut corps have been trained in Star City, Russia's equivalent to the astronaut training facilities in Houston. Vick of GlobalSecurity. org believes that the mission will include a range of activities of military significance. Those may include efforts by the first taikonaut or taikonauts to demonstrate their expertise at using powerful cameras to gather images of the Earth's surface and other instruments to intercept telecommunication signals. (*Houston Chronicle*, 2003/10/12)

Chinese women traditionally are confined indoors for a month after delivering a baby on the grounds that they are particularly susceptible to various gynecological diseases in this period. During the maternity month, *maternity matron*, usually married women already having their own kids, are hired to take care of the newborn and the mother.

The Chinese character 颜 (*yan*) refers to people's face, with an extended meaning for the look, or the physical appearance of someone or something. So *appearance index* is a term recently coined to measure the good-looking or the value of beauty in society. Someone or something that ranks high on the *appearance index* doesn't have to look beautiful, but must be at least cool, trendy and decent.

*Leftover woman* ( *sheng nü* ) could be defined as an urban, educated woman over age 27 who is single. Here is an example from BBC Online.

> Still, she knows that these days, single, urban, educated women like her in China are called "sheng nü" or "leftover women"—and it stings. She feels pressure from her friends and her family, and the message gets hammered in by China's state-run media too. (2013/2/21, http://www.bbc.com/news/)

One of the hot Internet buzzwords in 2014 is *budget husband*, which refers to those men who are average or even mediocre in all the possible aspects but are extremely reliable and can somewhat promise stability for women.

The term *straight man cancer*, also coined in 2014, refers to chauvinist, judgmental behavior and language that propels sexist double standards or belittles women. Here is an example from *The Telegraph Online*.

> A term trending in China at the moment has got feminists hopeful about the future of equality in the country. "Straight man cancer", a Chinese take on "male chauvinist pig", has been leveled at men who make disparaging remarks against women. The term, which started to circulate last year, recently moved into the mainstream when a famous Chinese scholar, Zhou Guoping, posted on microblogging platform Weibo that women are beautiful when they're cleaning the house or feeding babies. An online storm ensued. Zhou was diagnosed with the so-called disease and quickly apologised. (2015/3/13, http://www.telegraph.co.uk)

## 5.5 Summary

The global expansion of English as a vehicular language for

international and intercultural communication has fundamentally challenged the ideology of native-speakerism. English is no longer owned solely by those of the Anglo-Saxon heritage but shared by bilingual and multilingual language users all over the world in different locations and for different purposes. Over the past two decades, the speed and scope of China's economic development have indeed been remarkable and its effects have been felt globally. China's emergence as the world's fastest growing marketplace will undoubtedly influence the amount of contact English has with Chinese languages and the manner in which contact develops. In the context of World English, there is a good reason to guess that Chinese words could play a significant role in the future of English and borrowing and assimilation of loans from Chinese will be more frequent and more extended. Chinese have the largest number of English speakers now. History has taught us that when a critical mass of speakers adopts a new language and remains in unbroken contact with those for whom it is a mother tongue, the new group's native language can play a prominent role in the evolution of their adopted language. "What is certain about future borrowings from Chinese is that borrowing will continue to reflect the nature of contact between Chinese and English speakers." (Moody, 1996: 417) As commodities in supermarkets all around the world can be easily found to have a tag that reads "Made in China", it is predicted that in the future, there will certainly more words coming into English with the identity as "Made in China".

# Chapter 6 Conclusion

Any language, under appropriate circumstances, borrows lexical material from other languages, usually absorbing the exotic items or translating them into native equivalents. Linguistic borrowing is one of the most silent consequences of language contact. The continuous flux of loanwords is the essence of a living language. Loanwords have been a fascinating topic in scholarly work, and a great deal of research on loanwords has been carried out from diverse points of view. This book focuses on the Chinese words which have been borrowed into the vocabulary of English. It also examines the new phase of Chinese borrowings into the English language in the context of World English.

English stands out among languages around the world for its highly heterogeneous vocabulary made up of words borrowed from many Western as well as Eastern languages. It has already borrowed from over 350 languages in the past, and it continues to draw on these same resources. The wider the range of English use the more likely it will absorb foreign words. English and Chinese are typologically distinct languages, yet the differences between them have in no way impeded mutual borrowing. Although the number of loanwords from Chinese to English is relatively low, they should not be neglected.

Chinese loanwords have resulted from contact between the Chinese and the English languages brought about by the coming of English-speaking people to China and the migration of Chinese-speaking people to English-speaking parts of the world. For historical, political, social and many other reasons, extent of contact between English and Chinese varies from area to area in China. Chinese loanwords came from multiple primary sources, including Mandarin, Cantonese, Amoy and several other Chinese dialects. Some words are passed through another language of transmission, Japanese in particular, before they are borrowed into English.

When Chinese words are adopted into English, the convenient way is to take the sound directly or make some changes for the ease of pronunciation in English. Many words were borrowed into the English language as phonetic loans through the influx of immigrants. New expressions created by translating the Chinese characters into phonetically corresponding or similar morphemes in English. Phonetic loans account for the major percentage in the sum of Chinese loanwords in English.

Borrowings from Chinese languages constitute several semantic fields which reflect the nature of contact between Chinese and English speakers and the complex patterns of cultural contact between China and the West across centuries. Chinese loanwords cover almost all aspects of life, such as food, clothing, arts and crafts, architecture, aesthetics, economics, education, medicine, philosophy, politics, religion and so on. Subject matter determines the choice and integration of lexis to some extent.

English and other European languages such as French, Italian, German, Spanish, Dutch all belong to the Indo-European family, and are closely related culturally and geographically. Chinese and English are in completely different language families, and China and the Inner Circle countries are also thousands of miles apart, in terms of both physical distance and sociolinguistic distance. This may be one of the reasons that Chinese loanwords are fewer in number compared with languages spoken in Western countries. Nowadays, however, geography is no longer so decisive in linguistic contacts because of the development of modern means of communications. An obvious impact of globalization is that language communities will have more contact with each other (Wright, 2004). As global integration develops, cultural and language contact has been intensified in depth as well as breadth. Mere rejection of or assimilation between different cultures has been replaced by the thirst of mining other cultures to enrich one's own culture. The high speed Internet connects people all over the world, and cyber expressions have accelerated the process of language contact and vocabulary assimilation. Usually a new word will be copied immediately after its first use. Since China has opened up to the outside world, and because of its growing international importance, coverage in the media is increasing and because of growing familiarity with things Chinese, phonetic loans and direct translations of Chinese terms and phrases are more and more impinging on the consciousness of the English-speaking world. China English is becoming an acknowledged variety of world English. Vocabulary associated with unique Chinese features will enhance the expressiveness of China English.

A large number of Chinese loanwords were analyzed and discussed in this book and the data was collected from various channels. However, the analyses did not come in depth concerning the phonological aspects of loanwords. Chinese and English have different phonological systems. This involves looking at some very complicated issues. Some words are pronounced and transcribed according to the once commonly used Wade system, which is quite different from the current Chinese *Pinyin*.

It needs to be pointed out that the words of Chinese origins examined in this book are of different phases if we regard the term loanword as a dynamic concept. Some words are conformed to the conventions of English and have lost their Chinese identity. Some words, not completely naturalized, have become more familiar, especially through exposure in the media and occur unmarked. A small number of them are merely nonce borrowings, restricted to Chinese contexts and used in novels or journalistic works with a view to giving stylistic flavor. Because of the lack of research materials for certain segments, there is often a good deal of subjectivity involved in deciding whether one etymology is more convincing than another.

As Cannon (1987: 205) points out, "Chinese has significantly contributed lexical items and semantic conceptions to English which are usually not geographically or stylistically restricted and which are often a part of general international English. The total loans and productivity of naturalized Chinese forms are far more numerous and varied than has been known, so that scholars need to show a much greater appreciation for such items when composing histories of English in the future." What is certain about future borrowings from Chinese is that English as a global language will not be complete without Chinese elements. We should not adopt the "wait and see" attitude. Instead, we need to actively promote Chinese key concepts and terms. As to the research in this field, we believe an integration of linguistic, historical and cultural approaches to Chinese loanwords in English will be a promising and worthwhile endeavor.

## References

Algeo, J. (1990). Borrowing. In E. G. Polome (ed.), *Research Guide on Language Change*. Berlin: Mouton de Gruyter. 409-413.

Algeo, J. (2010). *The Origins and Development of the English Language*. (6th ed). Boston: Wadsworth.

Bliss, A. (1966). *A Dictionary of Foreign Words and Phrases in Current English*. New York: Dutton.

Bloomfield, L. (1933). *Language*. New York: Henry Holt and Co.

Campbell, L. & M. J. Mixco. (2007). *A Glossary of Historical Linguistics*. Edinburgh: Edinburgh University Press.

Cannon, G. (1987). Dimensions of Chinese Borrowings in English. *Journal of English Linguistics*, (2): 200-206.

Cannon, G. (1988). Chinese Borrowings in English. *American Speech*, (1): 3-33.

Cannon, G. (1990). Sociolinguistic Implications of Chinese Language Borrowings in English. *International Journal of the Sociology of Language*, (1): 41-55.

Cannon, G. (1992). Malay (sian) borrowings in English. *American*

*Speech*, 67 (2): 134-162.

Carroll, D. (1973). *The Dictionary of Foreign Terms in the English Language*. New York: Hawthorn Books.

Chan, M. (1983). Of hongs and tongs and all that jazz: A note on lexical borrowing from Chinese in English with special reference to Hong Kong. *Journal of the Royal Asiatic* Society Hong Kong Branch, 23: 62-90.

Chan, M. & H. Kwok. (1985). *A Study of Lexical Borrowing from Chinese into English with Special Reference to Hong Kong*. Hong Kong: Center of Asian Studies, University of Hong Kong.

Coe, A. (2009). *Chop Suey: A Cultural History of Chinese Food in the United States*. Oxford: Oxford University Press.

Crystal, D. (1995). *The Cambridge Encyclopedia of the English Language*. Cambridge: Cambridge University Press.

Crystal, D. (2003). *English as a Global Language* (2nd edn.). Cambridge: Cambridge University Press.

Crystal, D. (2008). Two thousand million? *English Today*, 24: 3-6.

Davies, D. (2013). *Varieties of Modern English: An Introduction.* London: Routledge.

Davis, E. L. (2005). *Encyclopedia of Contemporary Chinese Culture*. London: Routledge.

Delahunty, A. (1997). *The Oxford Dictionary of Foreign Words and Phrases*. Oxford: Oxford University Press.

Doi, S. (2014). The naturalisation process of the Japanese loanwords found in the Oxford English Dictionary. *English Studies*, 95(6): 674-699.

Dunton-Downer, L. (2010). *The English Is Coming! —How One*

*Language Is Sweeping the World*. New York: Touchstone.

Durkin, P. (2014). *Borrowed Words: A History of Loanwords in English*. Oxford: Oxford University Press.

Ehrlich, E. (1990). *The Harper Dictionary of Foreign Terms* (3rd edn.). New York: Harper & Row.

Foster, B. (1968). *The Changing English language*. Harmondsworth: Penguin Books.

Grant, A. (2009). Loanwords in British English. In M. Haspelmath and U. Tadmor (eds.), *Loanwords in the World's Languages: A Comparative Handbook*. Berlin: De Gruyter Mouton.

Gu, Y. (2009). Chinese. In K. Brown & S. Ogilvie (eds.), *Concise Encyclopedia of Language of the World*. Oxford: Elsevier.

Haugen, E. (1950). The analysis of linguistic borrowing. *Language*, 26(2): 210-231.

Haugen, E. & M. Mithun (2003). Borrowing: Overview. In W. J. Frawley et al. (eds.), *International Encyclopedia of Linguistics* (2nd edn.). New York: Oxford University Press.

Hockett, C. F. (ed.). (1979). *The Life and Growth of Language by W. D. Whitney*. New York: Dover Publications

Hoffer, B. L. (2005). Language borrowing and the indices of adaptability and receptivity. *Intercultural Communication Studies* 14, 53-72.

Jackson, H. & E. Z. Amvela. (2007). *Words, Meaning and Vocabulary: An Introduction to Modern English Lexicology*. London: Continuum.

Jespersen, O. (1922). *Language: Its Nature, Development and Origin*. London: G. Allen & Unwin.

Kachru, B. B. (1986). *The Alchemy of English: The Spread, Functions and Models of Non-native Englishes*. Oxford: Pergamon Press.

Kachru, B. B. (2005). *Asian Englishes: Beyond the Canon*. Hong Kong: Hong Kong University Press.

Kachru, B. B. (2006). English: World Englishes. In K. Brown et al. (eds.), *Encyclopedia of Language and Linguistics* (2nd edn.). Oxford: Elsevier.

Kuiper, K. (ed.). (2011). *The culture of China*. New York: Britannica Educational Publishing.

Lehmann, W. P. (1962). *Historical Linguistics: An Introduction*. New York: Holt, Rinehart and Winston.

Liu, Haiming. 2009. Chop suey as imagined authentic Chinese food: The culinary identity of Chinese restaurants in the United States. *Journal of Transnational American Studies*, (1): 1-36.

Manser, M. H. (2008). *The Facts on File Dictionary of Foreign Words and Phrases* (2nd edn.). New York: Facts On File, Inc.

McArthur. T. (1987). The English Languages, *English Today*, (11): 9-13.

McArthur, T. (1992). *The Oxford Companion to the English Language*. Oxford: Oxford University Press.

Metcalf, A. (1999). *The World in So Many Words—A Country-by-Country Tour of Words That Have Shaped Our Language*. Boston: Houghton Mifflin Company.

Mitter, R. (2008). *Modern China: A Very Short Introduction*. Oxford: Oxford University Press.

Moody, A. J. (1996). Transmission languages and source languages of Chinese borrowings in English. *American Speech*, 71 (4): 405-420.

Morris, E. E. (2011). *Austral English: A Dictionary of Australasian Words, Phrases and Usages*. Cambridge: Cambridge University Press.

Mullany, L. & P. Stockwell. (2010). *Introducing English Language—A Resource Book for Students*. London: Routledge.

Poplack, S. & D. Sankoff. (1984). Borrowing: The synchrony of integration. *Linguistics*, 22: 99-135.

Richards, J. C. & R. Schmidt. (2010). *Longman Dictionary of Language Teaching and Applied Linguistics* (4th edn.). London: Longman.

Roberts, J. A. G. (2002). *China to Chinatown: Chinese Food in the West*. New York: Reaktion Books.

Sapir, E. (2002). *Language: An Introduction to the Study of Speech*. Beijing: Foreign Language Teaching and Research Press.

Seargeant, P. (2005). Globalisation and reconfigured English in Japan. *World Englishes*, 24: 309-319.

Seidlhofer, B. (2004). Research perspectives on teaching English as a lingua franca. *Annual Review of Applied Linguistics*, 24: 209-239. Cambridge: Cambridge University Press.

Seng, G. Y. & L. S. Lai (2010). Global Mandarin. In V. Viniti (ed.), *Globalization of Language and Culture in Asia: The Impact of Globalization Processes on Language*. London: Continuum.

Serjeantson, M. S. (1935). *A History of Foreign Words in English*. London: Kegan Paul.

Shibatani, M (2009). Japanese. In K. Brown & S. Ogilvie (eds.),

*Concise Encyclopedia of Language of the World*. Oxford: Elsevier.

Stockwell, R. & D. Minkova. (2001). *English Words: History and Structure*. Cambridge: Cambridge University Press.

Thomason, S. & T. Kaufman. (1988). *Language Contact, Creolization and Genetic Linguistics*. Berkeley: University of California Press.

Thomason, S. G. (2001). *Language Contact*. Edinburgh: Edinburgh University Press.

Trask, R. L. (1996). *Historical Linguistics*. London: Arnold.

Trask, R. L. (2007). *Language and Linguistics: The Key Concepts* (2nd edn.). London: Routledge.

Tsou, B. K. (1975). On the linguistic covariants of cultural assimilation. *Anthropological Linguistics*, 17 (9): 445-465.

Varchaver, M. & F. L. Moore (2001). *The Browser's Dictionary of Foreign Words and Phrases*. New York: John Wiley & Sons, Inc.

Weinreich, U. (1953). *Languages in Contact: Findings and Problems*. Berlin: Mouton de Gruyter.

Winford, D. (2003). *An Introduction to Contact Linguistics*. Oxford: Blackwell.

Wright, S. (2004). *Language Policy and Language Planning: From Nationalism to Globalization*. New York: Palgrave Macmillan.

Zuckermann, G. (2003). Language contact and globalisation: The camouflaged influence of English on the world's languages—with special attention to Israeli (sic) and Mandarin. *Cambridge Review of International Affairs*, 16 (2): 287-307.

陈胜利:《英语中的汉语借词研究——接触语言学视角》,苏州大学 2014 年博士论文。

陈新仁:《当代中国的英语使用及其本土化研究》,北京大学出版社 2012 年版。

郭鸿杰:《英语对现代汉语的影响——语言认知研究法》,上海交通大学出版社 2005 年版。

胡兆云:《语言接触与英汉借词研究》,山东大学出版社 2001 年版。

梁慧敏:《英语词典中的汉语音译借词》,载《语文建设通讯》2006 年第 3 期。

刘法公:《英语借自汉语的外来语考释》,载《山东外语教学》1991 年第 1 期。

汪榕培、常骏跃:《英语词汇中汉语借词的来源》,载《四川外语学院学报》2001 年第 4 期。

许爱军:《英语中的汉语借词及其生存状态》,载《华北电力大学学报(社会科学版)》2009 年第 2 期。

张逸、蔡静:《从英语词典中的汉语词汇看文化多样化和语言借用》,载《国外外语教学》2005 年第 4 期。

张勇先:《英语发展史》,外语教学与研究出版社 2014 年版。

郑声滔:《源于汉语的英语词汇》,载《现代外语》1985 年第 3 期。